Praise for

MW00620782

WHOOPS! I FORGOT TO ACHIEVE MY POTENTIAL

by Maggie Huffman

"I remember, in college, writing a list of all the things I wanted to accomplish by the time I was 30. I kept that list until my 30th birthday. Let's just say, I hadn't accomplished much from my list. AT ALL. And the realization of this sent me into one hell of a quarter life crisis, where I marinated in a near fatal depression for years. I wish I would have had access to this book back then. Maggie's irreverent, smart, non-BS approach to life-navigation is spot on. Thanks to Maggie's experience and wisdom, change management is not just for big business any more, and that's a very good thing. If you've ever compared yourself to a list of things you were "supposed to do" and fallen short, this is your new bible."

Amy Pearson
Queen of Radical Results
http://www.livebrazen.com

"WHOOPS! I Forgot to Achieve My Potential is a FUNNY, loving, and completely intriguing read. It is much more than a book; it is a voyage. There is insightful, explorative, and juicy content that takes you into the depths of your own being. There were at least 25 moments while reading when I thought, "Oooo I need to tell _____ to read this book," and every time it was a different person that came to my mind. Maggie touches on so much magic, and I know this book will help many.

If you woke up this morning and thought, "what the he** am I doing with my life," allow this book to give you the answers. If you find yourself thinking "there has to be more," allow this book to guide you to the more you seek. If you know you were put here for a purpose, yet not breathing it every day, this book is for you.

I am thankful to Maggie for standing in a place of vulnerability, and shining her story for all to see so that the rest of the world can learn from it. I celebrate Maggie and her 1st book, and am honored she is a part of my journey and my heart tribe!"

Gina Rossi
Feng Shui Practitioner
Intuitive Counselor
www.ginanicole.net

"Wherever you are in life, the question comes up, "What happened?" Maggie Huffman's *Whoops! I Forgot to Achieve My Potential* (2015 Difference Press) acknowledges your experience, yet moves onward to the essential: "What is possible for me? Can I find balance? Meaning? And how?"

Speaking of which, some circles of life coaching focus on ontology (to use the fancy word)—who and how we are *being*, rather than simply what we are doing. There's a reason Krista Tippet's breakthrough radio syndication success changed its name from "Speaking of Faith" to "On Being." There's a reason *Tikkun's* editor, Rabbi Michael Lerner, spotlights the U.S. psyche in *The Left Hand of God* (2007): we are in chronic spiritual crisis because the larger culture keeps telling us we are valuable to the degree we are useful, while every wisdom tradition, religion, or truly human sensibility tells us we are valuable, period. Huffman targets that split for repair.

This book is different. Yes, it offers tools for where you are right now. It's also a blast—fun and playful with life's drama. At times you can almost hear the text whispering to *On the Waterfront's* (Kazan, 1954) cynical protagonist, Terry (Marlon Brando), as he mumbles, "I coulda been a contender. I coulda been somebody..." OK, so you're not that guy or gal. But most of us have drifted some in that direction. Huffman's book offers a map to your own landscape of potential, meaning, authenticity, and transformation. Start now; that's all we have.

Whoops! lives right along the multiplicity of paths that our Spirit Road Radio adapted from Frederick Buechners's wonderful description of vocation (in *Wishful Thinking: A Theological ABC*), as our broadcasts invited folks to meet us "at the crossroads where your joy and the world's needs meet." Huffman knows that territory. She's a wise, friendly, down-to-earth—and experienced—guide on that journey. Which sometimes is not only all we've got, but also pretty much all we can ask for."

Rick Bernardo
Assistant Professor (Management Ethics/Organizational Leadership) St. Mary's University of MN Producer, Spirit Road Radio

"Whoops! I Forgot to Achieve My Potential by Maggie Huffman—A down-to-earth guide, allowing us to find balance while working through life's transitions.

I thoroughly enjoyed reading this life-changing book! Such a pleasure to read the stories of corporate world frustrations and knowing there is light at the end of the tunnel. Having been in many of the same situations as Maggie, it was easy for me to relate to her problems. Many of us feel like we screwed-up our lives, missed our potential, or just are unhappy. Sometimes a do-over in life is needed. Maggie guides you through it all with humor, sensitivity, and spirituality.

There are no coincidences in life... having this book at this time made sense. Like so many others, I am now living a life I never would have imagined. Since my car accident, life has been very different for me. Good, but different. I never realized just how unhappy I was in my previous career. This book really digs deep. It helps you work through who you are, how to love yourself, and how to get where you want to be. Maggie's words truly struck a chord with me. It is so inspiring to know it's never too late to achieve your potential."

Thank you so much Maggie! xoxo

Brandi Kay
Psychic Medium
Blog: www.thehealedspirit.com
Website: www.bkaymedium.com

"WHOOPS! I Forgot to Achieve My Potential is written by Maggie Huffman, a graduate of the Institute for Integrative Nutrition, where she completed a cutting edge curriculum in holistic nutrition, taught by the world's leading experts in health and wellness. I recommend you read this book and be in touch with Maggie to see how she can help you successfully achieve your goals in life."

Joshua Rosenthal, MScEd
Founder/Director, Institute for Integrative Nutrition

"Maggie Huffman's breezy style has intention and invitation woven through it: there is transforming purpose here, people!

Maggie offers practical steps to discover the authentic life, the one that feels true and balanced from your tippy toes to the top of your hair. Sure, this is a book that you read but it's more a book that you "do."

Maggie writes with an easy mix of humor and practical wisdom, just the kind of company you want to keep on this journey. I laughed quite a few times reading this—and so did my husband (I was reading it aloud to him on a long car trip). Other times, I got real quiet as a phrase shone like a beacon off the page right into me.

For those of us who may be waking up and wandering lost in Dante's wood—at whatever age it comes!—Maggie's "good news" is that transformation is a process available to anyone anytime. And she makes clear in her steps that it is not about struggle and pain but curiosity and love. Oh yeah, we can go for that :)"

Kimberly Ayers
Travel curator, broadcast journalist, front-row alto occasional contributor at www.thecaliforniareport.org

"You don't have to be in need of a complete overhaul to benefit from Maggie's wisdom and practical approach. But lucky you if you do. She makes finding and achieving one's potential—or facets thereof—a journey that is easily accessible and ultimately enjoyable.

Through her wide-ranging specific examples and compelling personal story you will see that you always have potential, and it is never too late."

RuthE. Wells
TheGreenDiva.GPDB.com

Becky—

Hope 2016 is everything you want!

Maggie Hoffman

WHOOPS!

I FORGOT TO ACHIEVE MY POTENTIAL

By Maggie Huffman

Dedication

For Katie, my sister and best friend.

May we never run out of tea, stories, desserts, bike rides or other happy things to share.

Table of Contents

Act 4. THE SET UP FOR THE SEQUEL

EPILOGUE

Chapter 1.

Introduction

"If I had an hour to solve a problem I'd spend 55 minutes thinking about the problem and 5 minutes thinking about solutions."

~ Albert Einstein

So why did you pick up this book? Because something happened in your life that made you start thinking. And they weren't happy thoughts that had you sitting and reflecting on all of your accomplishments with a warm glow of satisfaction. No, the thoughts probably started like a little earworm — a phrase or an image or the refrain of a song from your youth that reminded you: "Oh, I used to want to be ____." And it started repeating and becoming louder. "I used to have dreams. I used to believe I was going to do big things. I was going to be important. I used to have *potential*." And then, bam, it's a full on attack. It keeps you up at night or wakes you up with its persistent shouting. You look at young people who still have their dreams and you realize that you are *jealous* of their hope, their belief in themselves and their potential. You wish you could start over (of course, knowing everything you know now) and get a fresh shot at fulfilling your potential. You find yourself thinking about making changes... but is it too late? What could you possibly do *now*, at this late stage in the game? And what is your true purpose, really and truly? When you're feeling overly dramatic and quite sorry for yourself, you wonder if it's all worth it. Of course, you have obligations, people who need you, things to do. You've made your bed, so just lie in it, right? And it all feels a little self-indulgent to be spending this much time worrying and wondering about your own life, especially when you're so *busy* doing the stuff life needs you to do.

But still, you wake up in the middle of the night. You find yourself dreaming of winning the lottery and starting over. You google all kinds of random topics, looking for inspiration. You wish, wish, wish for your fairy godmother to appear and wave her magic wand, getting you an audition for *The Voice*, or an apprenticeship for your dream job, or enough money to travel and write your adventure book, or a Tim Gunn makeover, or (insert your dream here). Or maybe you just want your fairy godmother to tell you what you should do and how to do it, because you're tired of making all the big decisions for everyone else when you really don't give a crap about all of that anymore. *What about me?*

By this time, you realize you're a bit of a basket case, you've completely convinced yourself that there's no hope, that it's too late, you'll never be who you thought you would be, your life is over, so just stop whining and make dinner. And dinner should be gruel and worms, because that's all you deserve for being such a humongous failure.

What happened to start this whole roller coaster ride anyway? Was it a significant life event, like a divorce, loss of a loved one, getting laid off from your job (a.k.a. being "made redundant"), kids going off to college, or something else big that just forced you to hold a spotlight on your life?

Or was it something more subtle, like finding a box of mementos from your younger days, or reconnecting with someone from your past on Facebook? Was it a reunion? Was it a child thinking about their career? Was it celebrating a friend's promotion or gallery opening or wedding? Was it finishing in the middle of the pack in a race? Was it realizing that you are no longer the youngest overachiever in the room? (It was for me.) Was it looking at the new kid's resume — a *child* really — and comparing it to your paltry list of accomplishments?

Maybe, once upon a time, you were good at too many things to choose and you couldn't find a path that integrated them all, or even choose what was most important to you. So you settled in by accident to the life you have now… and then, bam, one of your other potential roads decided to sit up and slap you in the face.

Whatever happened, it was a miracle. Really. You are one of the lucky ones! I know it doesn't feel like it right now, because you are sitting in a simmering pot of discontent seasoned with bitterness, resentment, despair, hopelessness and a sense of failure. Or some such thing. If you're not there yet, don't worry — if you don't address it willingly it'll keep coming back. Sure, you can anesthetize yourself with business and distractions; numb yourself with food, drink, drugs, gambling, shopping or any of a number of destructive behaviors. You can fill your time with so much busy-ness or business that you don't have any time left to think. But, guess what? Eventually you'll wake up in the middle of the night thinking, "Oh my God — it's too late! What happened to all my **potential!**"

"Maggie, how can you say that this misery is a miracle?" Well, the obvious answer is that I can say it because it happened to me, and finding my way out was the best thing that ever happened to me. I'll tell you about that in a minute.

The less obvious truth is that the earworm of discontent is the seed of hope. That seed will grow until it is so big you can't avoid it anymore. That seed is your true potential. I'm gonna play with this metaphor a little. The seed is like a pinecone in the forest. It needs some miserable conditions - a little fire, a little freezing, a little fertilizing (another word for bullshit) and a little water to finally decide to become a seedling. I could go on until we get to the mighty pine standing tall in the forest, but I've already stretched this a bit too much for my taste. I bet you know where I'm going, anyway.

Look, something inside you is waking up. It doesn't feel good. But you have the opportunity to deal with it now. You know what? It's not too late. It's never too late. You don't believe me. Yet. But you will. You still have tons of potential — an amazing, exciting life full of potential. Okay, maybe you can't be the youngest person to discover a new life form in the Amazon. Maybe you can't be an Olympic gymnast. Yes, you do have to face the fact that there are some things you can't and won't be — so they aren't part of the potential you. **Get over it!** Admit it, grieve and mourn and move on. Why? Because there is so much more to you, so much that you *can* do and be! And you probably want to get going, right? Oh. You're not sure where to go. Okay, hang on. We'll deal with that, too. Remind me to get back to that, okay?

So, again, how is this earworm of discontent so wonderful? Because it really feels pretty miserable. And it's getting louder.

It's fantastic because it is your real self — your highest and best self — calling out to you in a loving voice, saying "Hey! Wake Up! Get off your ass!" Yes, that voice does sound a little like the squawk of a blue jay.

This is as good a time as any for the woo-woo disclaimer. This book is fundamentally based on the truth that you are a spiritual being in a physical body, that you have an eternal element within you and that you have all kinds of access to the wisdom of a higher self, if you choose to acknowledge it. We will be talking about souls and spirits and intuition and all kinds of "magical" stuff like that. And we will be using it for good — for your higher good. And you're going to discover a few of your own superpowers. If all that offends you, I'm sorry (for you).

By the way, I use the term "woo-woo" with a lot of affection. I know that skeptics like to use it with a sarcastic or scathing tone of voice. I figure I should just reclaim it for all of us who need a good catchall term. So I use it lovingly, as in "love me some woo-woo."

I'll pick up the thread of my own story now. I was an amazing kid. I was really smart, pretty motivated and more than a tad competitive. I skipped grades. I left high school to go to college — didn't bother to graduate. Got a full scholarship. I finished college in three years, including studying abroad. I had three majors (music, languages and religious studies). I went into grad school able to legally drink by one month. I was in seminary in Berkeley, California. I wanted to be a minister and, at that time, it was still an unusual career choice for a *"girl."* I was going to have a musical ministry as a political activist. I was so young and so full of potential. Everyone believed in me, and they knew I was going to do great things, important things. I knew I was destined to have an impact on the world.

In my last year of grad school, my youngest brother was in a motorcycle accident, and he broke his neck. C-4/5. A quadriplegic. I dropped everything to support him in rehab and then put my life on pause to be his caregiver as he transitioned back home and beyond. I worked, but the jobs were just to make money — not a career. I did finish my degree, but my heart was no longer in becoming a minister. There were other reasons for that choice, too, so it really did work out.

The life expectancy for a quadriplegic at that time was 5–10 years. I loved my brother and my family very much, so it was an easy choice to spend 5–10 years living near him and supporting him in all kinds of ways. After about 10 years, he was still alive, and we realized that he wasn't going to die anytime soon and he actually had a pretty happy and independent life. So I needed to get started on my career.

Well, here I was — this young prodigy who was now in her early thirties — still pretty young, though, right? I decided that I needed a career, not just a job. So I looked around. I lived in Sonoma, in the heart of the wine country. I said, "What can I do if I want to make a good living here?" Duh, work in the wine industry. So I got a job as a temp at a wonderful wine company. They saw my potential and hired me full-time, and I started climbing the ladder. I was promoted nine times in three years. I went from temp to director in six years. It wasn't what I had originally planned for myself, but it was good and I was challenged and I was successful. Corporate stuff happened (recessions, acquisitions, restructures, job moves, promotions, etc.). I had lots of amazing opportunities and experiences and built up a really great set of skills for myself as a leader of business-type transformations.

But, gradually, I began to hear the earworm of discontent. Remember the earworm? That incredibly annoying song fragment that you find yourself humming or whistling? It keeps repeating until you can't get it out of your head. It's usually something like Disney's *It's a Small World*. You now have that in your head. You're welcome! The earworm of discontent is just like that — an annoying emotion that you can't get out of your head. Mine started out softly — as frustration because I wasn't able to accomplish more. I worked for an Australian-owned company, and had hit the not-so-invisible glass ceiling. I became more and more frustrated with my work. No matter what my role, I felt like I was the Mistress of Fixing Broken Shit. I wasn't really doing anything that made a difference. I felt like I wasn't really helping people. It wasn't what I was meant to do. It sure wasn't *enough*. But I didn't know what I was meant to do anymore. And what could I do? I was no longer the young whiz kid with so much potential. I was almost never the youngest person in *any* room. Was it too late?

I thought it was probably too late to realize my *full* potential, but maybe if I tried harder I could still burst through a bit higher in this same realm. But I found myself eating more. Drinking more wine. Working ridiculous hours. Doing everything myself, instead of delegating to my staff. I spent lots of money buying things. I had the newest gadgets the day they came out. I had multiples of everything. I ordered things online so I would have presents waiting for me when I came home. I kept looking outside myself for the thing that would make me feel better. Of course, it didn't work.

But maybe there was still something I could do that would make me happier. I started going back to some of the things I had done earlier in my life. I got a coach. I discovered Aura-Soma. I started trying new things. I made time for new things. I rekindled my spiritual practices.

Then my mom died. And one of my best friends died some months later. There's a beautiful story here, which I will come back to later in the book. That was my really big wakeup call. As I was grieving, I realized I did not want to waste anymore of my life doing things that didn't really matter, that didn't make me happy. I wanted no regrets. I really began exploring more things, testing out possibilities and dreaming about what I wanted to do. I started building a part-time coaching and consulting practice — which I loved and found tremendously exciting.

Ironically, things at work began to suck more and more. It was just hard, and it was going to get harder before it got better. I was given the task of restructuring and laying people off (again). Woo hoo! Then I engineered my own layoff, and launched my full-time practice as a life coach. I'm happy now, and want to share my happiness with you. I know for a fact that if I hadn't had that earworm of discontent growing inside me, I would never have made the decisions I did. I would never have made the changes I did to get back on track, to discover and realign with my true purpose. And that's how I know the earworm of discontent is a miracle!

So, what's in this book? It's a map to take you on a journey to discover and reclaim your purpose and your potential. The goal? Simply to be the best *you* that you can possibly be. Life is not just about what you achieve, it's about who you are and how you live.

What's in this book? Hope. You know how it feels when you've been sick for a long time, running a fever, aching, no energy? And you know what it feels like when you start to get better — that glimmer of light when you realize. "Oh, this is what it feels like to feel *normal!*" That's hope. That's what is in this book. What awaits you on your journey is getting to rediscover yourself, sampling things to know what you like and what you don't like. You will awaken your taste buds for life and your curious palate. You will discover what it takes for you to make choices and take actions that get you back on the road to achieving your potential.

What will this journey require of you? The willingness to

• Be truly open to try new things (how do you know you don't like asparagus?)

• Give yourself what you need and want

• Find your super powers (step into your super hero suit)

• Acknowledge some kind of higher power

• Have fun and adventures (as you define them)

• Choose what works for you

If you are willing to do these things, you are ready to start this journey. I'm willing to go along with you. Let's get ready...

FIELD NOTES

Alarm clock: What happened in your life to wake you up?

Poke the pain: What kinds of things is your earworm saying? What's keeping you up at night?

📖✍ FIELD NOTES ✎📖

Dare to dream: What would you like to feel?
What do you want? Do you know?

Trigger words: desires, longing, yearning, craving,
hunger, passions, hopes, missing

Chapter 2.

Your Personal Change Management Strategy

"I love change. It's so easy and fun."

~ said no one, ever

So, let's just admit it right now. You want to make some changes. You probably don't know what they are yet, right? But you know something has got to change. You've got to get that earworm of discontent out of your head. You need to change the station, somehow. And you don't want the earworm to come back, so you want to make the change stick. If you are honest with yourself, you admit that you've tried to make changes in the past. Many of them haven't stuck, or you wouldn't be in this position. You would be a change-making machine, chugging your way down the road to Potentialtown, passing all kinds of milestones along the way. So let's take a few moments to set you up to be successful. That's the purpose of preparation — it's a set up.

The number one reason changes don't stick is that we don't pick something that fits us. There's no one-size-fits-all. Period. You are unique. Why would you expect that *just anything* off the shelf should fit you? That's unreasonable. Think back about some of the changes you've tried to make. Have you tried to change your eating plan? Go gluten-free, or Paleo or Atkins or South Beach or try the bacon diet (is that even a thing?)? Did you try to change your exercise regime by taking up barre? Give up Facebook for Lent? Did you try a new meditation practice? Did you try to jump on the bandwagon of the last or next big thing? You get the idea. How many of these things stuck? Most didn't, probably, because they don't fit. And that's totally okay. You should absolutely try anything that you think you might like, but don't commit to changing your life around it until you know it's a fit *for you*.

This journey that you are about to go on is all about trying new things to see if you like them before you choose to make a change. To make it sound more important, I will be calling it "research." But, really, it is just trying stuff out, sampling things, "tasting" things. Lots more on that in a minute....

The second biggest reason changes don't stick is that people don't do everything they can to set themselves up to succeed. They kind of throw themselves at the change and hope it works out. I think we can do better for you.

Over my long career of leading transformation projects in business settings, I've learned a lot about change management. Yes, it is a thing. In all my successful projects I invested heavily in change management practices — and the unsuccessful ones taught me what not to do. The wobbly ones taught me that you can usually get back on track if you employ some change management.

What is change management? It's actually a pretty rigorous discipline that runs through the duration of a project. It's about understanding the impact of change and putting things in place to prepare people and to ease the transition from the past to the future. Change management is all about helping people, so it makes sense that the learnings in a business setting would be transferrable to an individual's transformation, right? Here's what I learned:

Change is hard. It doesn't matter whether you like the excitement of change or want things to stay exactly as they are now. Change is still hard. And that is almost always a surprise! So be compassionate — with yourself and with the folks around you.

You need help. You want help. Get help when you can. Don't do it all yourself.

It takes a team. No one is an island. You need to get help (see above), but you don't want a bunch of individuals running around doing unconnected things. A team that is working together is a lot more effective, and it's a lot more fun. By the way, what happens to you affects your friends, family, co-workers, pets... they are all on your team.

Everyone has a role. If you involve your team, change doesn't happen *to* them, it happens *with* them. Keep them informed! Think about how things will impact your team, plan for it, talk about how it will affect them and their role. **The answer is not always training.** Training is the number one go-to solution for most people when they encounter a challenge: "Oh, I need some training." Sometimes you have to just *try*, and learn by trying. When you want to take up cooking, you don't just go to classes or watch cooking shows. You actually have to cook something and taste it and see if you like it. If you get stuck, you can always go get help.

Fun is huge. Laughter is great. You'll actually do it if it's fun, and it will be so much easier. "No pain, no gain" is *sooo* old school. Everything doesn't have to hurt. It's way better to take the fun route.

There's a process. There's always a process. The more you understand the process, the easier it is to go through it and to make course corrections. Processes have steps and milestones and pauses, a beginning and an end. Some processes repeat. Few processes are actually linear. Most processes can be improved. The real insight is that in a process, you take one step at a time. Make the steps manageable. Don't expect to finish overnight. Don't judge yourself for not being finished when you're still on a middle step.

Failure is part of the process. Failure is high-quality feedback. Most of the time we learn much more from our failures than we do from our successes. Everybody fails. Accept it. The sooner we get used to it, the easier it is to pick ourselves up, brush ourselves off and start again. Don't aim for failure, but accept it. Let people (this includes you!) fail without condemning them — don't deprive anyone of the lessons that can be learned.

Celebrate milestones and successes. Lots of projects don't celebrate when they hit an accomplishment or a milestone. And that just feels crappy. It feels really good to recognize a significant achievement and to celebrate it. It's kind of simplistic, but here's a pretty reliable test for good and evil, right and wrong: As long as your moral compass is sound, good *feels* good and light. Bad *feels* bad and heavy. So it's okay to do things that feel good, like celebrating.

Magic happens. When you do the things listed above as best as you can, something wonderful happens. You succeed. It may not look exactly like you imagined it would, but a lot of times it turns out better than you hoped.

Why did these change management things work in a business context? Because businesses are made up of people. What worked for me in business was taking a human, organic, heartfelt and sometimes even spiritual approach to projects. By the way, these practices don't work in an organization that doesn't know or value the people who make up the business (but that's just me venting, and that's another book).

I had a real "duh" moment when I realized that I had spent years being the conscience of my organizations and making sure humanity was present in all my projects. That realization helped me to really accept that the next step on my path was as a life coach. "Duh" moments are different from "aha" moments. "Aha" moments light you up with a new insight. "Duh" moments are kind of like "Wow, how did I miss that? It's so freakin' obvious now. Couldn't I have saved myself some time?" But don't discount the "duh" moments. They are invaluable... because you absolutely know that they are true.

Let's talk more about failure. A few paragraphs back, I put in a plug for learning from failure, and I meant it. I know you've learned a lot about yourself from failing and from succeeding. But this book is not about seeking more failure just so you can learn. How wretched would that be? Reminds me of the whole "suffering builds character" thing. We already have *enough* character, thank you very much. There are so many industries that have been built by keeping us in failure mode — in blame and shame — so that we are customers for life (can you say "diet"?) This book *is* about you taking control of your own success by 1) setting an intention to succeed, 2) preparing to succeed, 3) doing the shit you need to do to succeed, 3) trying stuff to see what works, 4) knowing when something doesn't work and 5) *hey! stop calling yourself a failure!*

Okay, now let's get to the real preparation. What do you need to do to get ready for this journey you are about to go on? You know, the one where you rekindle your enthusiasm for your life, get back in touch with your own sense of your potential and starting taking steps to achieve it? What's your personal change management strategy? I've figured out some of the big steps and list them below. You need to add your own personal tips and tricks.

Plan your approach. Are you going to read this book from cover to cover and then go back and do the exercises? Are you going to read the introduction and this chapter on preparation and then do the work in the next seven steps as you go along? Are you going to work with a coach? If you've worked with a coach before, are you going to coach yourself this time? If you haven't worked with a coach, are you going to see if working with me is a fit, either one-on-one or in a group program? I have a 12-week transformation program called Tapas For Your Soul. If you like this book, you'll probably like the program. If you know you want what this book offers, but you don't know if you can do it by yourself, the program is probably just the ticket. If you are really interested in the spiritual, woo-woo, magical and playful stuff, you will love the program. If you're at all interested, come on over to my site and schedule a call to talk with me and learn more, at www.TalktoMaggie.com

Set aside time and space for this process. Why? To actually get something done! Life happens. You know it does. We make time for the important things. What we don't make time for becomes unimportant — even if it really isn't! You are important, so make time. Allow yourself time. Put it in your calendar. Rearrange your day. Take a longer lunch. Get up earlier, stay up later. Whatever works for you. If you don't know what works, experiment until you find what works. (That last bit is so good that it almost requires a spoiler alert! You'll see why when we get to Chapter 6.) If you set aside time and space for this process, you are starting to create a ritual. There is something very special, even sacred, about taking the time and making the space to think and write about yourself and the things that are important to you. I so want you to be able to easily get in touch with your higher self and to hear what you have to say to yourself. Nothing works faster to make that happen than creating a sense of ritual and intention.

You'll need some tools. There will probably be — no, there's guaranteed to be — times when you come across something you don't want: fear, overwhelm, excuses, self-sabotage, resistance, lost of perspective, any number of scary sounding things. I almost hesitate to mention this here, because I don't want to scare you off by letting it slip that some of this might be hard. But you're going to find out anyway, and it's better if you aren't completely surprised. (See, this is me using change management stuff!) If you have tools that you've used in the past to help you get through difficult and stressful things (like change, for example), that's great. If you want more information on tools I've used with my clients, you can go to my website and get them. Some examples of tools I've had good success with are guided meditations, creative visualizations, breathing techniques, distance and perspective visualizations, and targeted playlists.

Other things you'll need:

A journal. You will be doing a lot of writing. Why? It

unblocks so many things. We can admit things to a journal that we don't often say out loud or even to ourselves. We discover thoughts, wisdom and inspiration we didn't even know we had. Journaling is a forum to release and heal, and to practice the art of self-expression. So pick a journal that you love - the appearance of the cover, the look and feel of the pages, the smell, the color... whatever it takes. But make sure it is a journal you will actually write in. I have this weird habit of buying journals that I love so much, but that I won't write in, because I want them to stay beautiful forever. I actually end up writing much more successfully in regular old notebooks. So get what will really work for you!

Access to the Internet. I probably don't even have to say this these days, but just in case you were planning on going through this process in a yurt in a remote desert, make sure the yurt has Wi-Fi. You'll want to research things. You'll become very curious and only Google will give you the quick answers to your questions. You'll certainly want to get to my website to check out some of my amazing bonus resources. You might want to create a Pinterest or Kifi account. You'll definitely want to check out some YouTube stuff (insert subliminal "watch Jimmy Fallon" message here). And, in fact, you'll probably want to check out my video for the first exercise, coming up in one paragraph.

Index or other blank cards. So, starting now, anytime you discover something insightful or true, I want you to write it down on a card. Just the truth in a sentence, not a whole paragraph or dissertation. It can be an "aha" moment, a "duh" moment, an insight, a revelation, a quote, an affirmation or anything that you find incredibly helpful. It just needs to be true for you. If you want to be fancy, you can buy a deck of blank game cards on Amazon or in a toy store.

But wait. What if you aren't sure how to tell for certain that something is true *for you*? That brings us to the first exercise.

EXERCISE

This exercise is a little bit woo-woo, but it has a strong scientific foundation, too. I don't apologize for using things that science hasn't explained yet!

You have an internal guidance system, a complex GPS. You started life with a natural bias toward health and energy. We have all kinds of ways to help us tell what is right for us, what is healthy and gives us good energy, what is true: pain (physical and emotional), joy, love, passion, discontent, happiness, fear, dreams, desires, emotions, moods — all are indicators giving us guidance. Intuition can be the major component of your inner guidance system. It is the ability to understand something immediately, without the need for conscious reasoning. It is the instantaneous integration of all the information we receive — at every level and from every source — into actionable wisdom. Everyone has intuition. It takes practice to relearn how to access, distinguish and rely on it.

The first location of intuition is your gut, the primary location for your "truth-o-meter." Intuition is how you know whether something is true or not without doing a bunch of intellectual work to prove it. There are actually different locations in your body for different kinds of intuition. But we're going to stick with this type for now.

There is so much new information on the brain/gut connection. I predict that the next big thing in science, nutrition and health is going to be focused on the micro-biome in our guts. In fact, there's so much good new information coming out about this every day, that if I try to do it justice today, it will probably be out of date by the time you read this. So Google it (*micro-biome or brain/gut connection*) and follow some of the more reliable sources if you want to satisfy your intellectual and scientific curiosity. Yes, that is part of this first exercise.

Here's the rest of the exercise. Think back to a time when you knew something was true — you just knew it in your gut. What did it feel like? Get really detailed in your description. What kind of sensation was it? Warm? Cool? Tingly? Electric? Did it spread through your body? Did you get goose bumps? How did the information travel to your brain? Did it turn into words? Try to relive that feeling so that you recognize it when it happens again.

Now that you know the feeling, practice using it as a lie detector. And you can get even better at it by using it in a more sophisticated way. Can you decipher the feelings that tell you "bullshit" or "danger"?

How do you know when something is true? I've got a video that leads you through this exercise. You can find it on my website via the link below.

Summing it all up:

- Change management is a thing.

- Personal change management should be a thing, so now it is.

- You are really important, so make time for this stuff.

- You'll want some tools to help when things get a bit hard.

- You need a journal, some blank cards and access to the Internet.

- Remember to write down on your cards any truths or insights you discover.

- You can get things from my website that will help you to get the most out of this book. You have to give me your email, and then I'll send you the link: www.WhoopsIForgotMyPotential.com.

NOTE: At the end of each chapter, there's a place for you to write. You probably already noticed, since I started in the previous chapter. You didn't? Pay attention! There are some questions to help you come up with your own personal observations and reactions to the content. In some chapters, there will also be a list of trigger words that might help provoke a deeper reaction, especially if you think about them in the context of the chapter.

By the way, this doesn't take the place of a journal! This is really a convenient place for you to capture your thoughts in context while still holding the book in your hands. A journal is very different than this book — it's bigger, more personal, maybe prettier, and of course, it's full of your words — not mine!

FIELD NOTES

What's your personal change management strategy?

What is your approach going to be?
Are you going to work through the book?

Will you augment with a coach or a group program?

What time & space are you going to set aside?
Will you create any rituals?

Who is on your team?

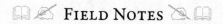

📖✍ FIELD NOTES ✍📖

What are your go-to tools for times of stress and over-whelm? Do you need some additional?

What else?

Intermission.

What's Coming Next

"I like to get people laughing. Then while their mouths are open, I pop in the truth."

~ Doug Adams, Humor and Religion Professor

We are ready to start your journey. Literally. So let me tell you what's coming up and what you'll be doing for the rest of the book. There are seven steps on your journey. Here they are:

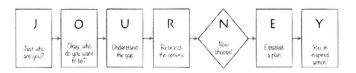

J — Just who are you?

O — Okay, now who do you want to be?

U — Understanding the gap between who you are and who you want to be

R — Researching your options (aka sampling stuff)

N — Now you choose

E — Establish a plan

Y — You, in inspired action!

How it works.

Each step has elements of learning, teaching, experiencing and practicing. I recommend you do the steps as you go along, and take the time you need for each step. Of course, you can read ahead, but reread the chapter when you are ready to *do* the chapter.

Big note: I'm presenting these steps as if they are linear, but they aren't. They are iterative. Especially the J-O-U-R steps. Hey, that's French for "day." I think that means that you'll actually be doing a little bit of each step every day. You should start researching your options right now. Try something new, to see if it works for you. You could start with this process!

Let's get started. Please try to have some fun among all the serious soul-searching, okay?

For you *Spamalot* fans, get ready for Act 3. Two, sir, two. Well, it's Chapter 3, anyway.

Chapter 3.

J — Just Who Are You?

"Because I knew you, I have been changed for good."

~ Elphaba and Glinda in *Wicked*, the musical

Let's start with some just-in-time learning. That's kind of a smart way of passing out the intellectual stuff in smaller bites so you don't get bored or tired of me. Plus, this way I can actually tie the ideas to the step you're working on and the exercises you're going to do.

Key Concepts

We are spiritual beings in a physical body.

We are not physical beings trying to attain some state of spirituality. We are already spiritual beings, and we are in this physical state of existence that is really an incarnation in time and space. We have access to our eternal, spiritual part. This is really important. If we get confused and think that we are physical beings trying to attain some spiritual state of perfection, we get all twisted around about our existence, our worth, who and what we have access to, and ultimately our purpose. We get really caught up in beliefs about having to earn our way into some state of grace. That leads to an enormous burden of shame and guilt about how we are finite, far from perfect and making mistakes all the time.

I can jump right up on a soap box about this — and it doesn't have to be very high — because I think this misunderstanding is the root of many of the problems with organized religion. I don't want to completely slam organized religion here, but I do need to say that it, like all other human endeavors, has its problems. Indulge me for a moment, please, and I'll try really hard to keep from ranting.

Have you ever loved a child? Of course you have. When he or she was born, didn't you say something like, "She's just perfect!" even though you knew she was just little and still had a lot of growing and developing to do? Looking at a newborn, can't you see the miracle that lives inside, the reflection of the spark of divinity? Can't you just see the spiritual being living inside that tiny little body, and all the hopes and dreams and, dare I say, *potential* that awaits that little life form? And that is before the little bean can do anything besides eat, breathe and poop!

We don't suddenly, or even gradually, change just because we grow older and start doing things. We don't morph from some totally innocent and infinitely valuable creation into something that now needs to earn its place in the universe. What changes is our perception and awareness. Oh, and our conditioning. Somewhere along the way, someone started a rumor that we were born from sin and we needed to earn our way back to being worthwhile. And the more that rumor spread, the more we believed it, until it just became part of the human fabric in our time. It almost doesn't matter what religion you are or whether you have any religious beliefs or not. We have all been conditioned to believe that guilt and shame are a part of the human condition, and that somehow we have to earn our way out to a higher level of existence. We just take it for granted. We aren't really aware that we don't have to believe that!

If you already don't believe that, thank you, and you can move on. If this is new to you, I'm asking you to consider the possibility that you really are a spiritual being, and you have worth just by being. You don't need to feel guilt and shame as your default setting.

The implications are massive. I'll leave it to much more eloquent theologians to handle the greater impacts. I want to talk about what it means for you and me.

Bottom line, it means you are enough. You don't have to go fulfill some mythical potential to be worthy of being alive, drawing breath or even being loved. *You are enough.* If you don't believe me, I want your first journal entry to be writing at least 100x — in red — these words: "I am enough." By the time you're done, you probably still won't believe me, but it will be a start. Just try it, okay?

So, does that mean you don't have to fulfill your potential? Yes. Yeppers. You betcha, that's what it means. It means that you can do it because you *want* to, not because you *have* to do it. I hope you get how different that feels. Compare and contrast: going to bed because you are tired and want to sleep versus going to bed because your mother said it was bedtime. See the difference? One way you love it, the other way you fight it. Even if it is good for you, and you might be a bit sleepy....

Here's the other thing. Human beings love doing stuff, making stuff, creating stuff, being good at stuff, trying new things. We really love trying things when we know that we don't have to be perfect the first time. We want to be amazing and fulfill our potential *simply because we want to be amazing.* We don't need the fear of failure or guilt or shame as a motivator. We want to find our purpose because that's how we are wired.

There's one other major implication, which I invite you to explore on your own, or you can investigate through my aforementioned transformation program, Tapas For Your Soul. The implication is that because you are a spiritual being on a physical quest (and not vice versa) you have access to all kinds of information, guidance and support from a host of other spiritual sources. To do a little name-dropping, the list includes but is not limited to God, your higher power, the Universe, Source, the creator, Angels, Spirit Guides, your eternal soul — to name just a few. They are waiting for you to reach out.

You are a complex, integrated being and, as such, you have many aspects. To be vibrantly alive, you need to recognize and be responsible for the care and feeding of the whole person. While you are really more complex than just these five aspects, they do work well as containers for the work of this journey: *mind, body, heart, spirit and soul*. Here's how I define them and how you'll be working with them on your journey.

Mind is your thoughts, intelligence and quest for knowledge. This is your intellectual processing, and the words in this book will first enter your mind. Some of the ideas might be familiar to you, but, hopefully, you will be engaged and challenged by a different perspective. The mind likes to be challenged.

Body is all things physical. In this journey, you will focus primarily on energy, food, movement, sleep, habits and health. The body has an astonishing ability to heal and maintain itself when properly supported. To support the natural healing processes, the body likes nutrition, hydration, rest and to be free of major toxins.

Heart is your emotional life. On your journey you will look at relationships, actions and feelings, with the blatant goal of feeling healthier, happier and joyous. And feeling love. Oh, and gratitude.

Spirit is your beliefs, practices and values. On your journey, you will need to examine your beliefs and update them to fit who you are now. This is about more than your religious, philosophical and spiritual beliefs — it's about your whole belief system, and includes what you believe about yourself, your place in the world, what you can and can't do — lots of the stuff in the belief container. You will look at various small practices to support being able to hear your spirit more clearly, and to trust it more fully — because trust is big, really big.

Soul is the eternal self — the spark of divinity that lives within us in this life. In this journey, you will focus on your creativity and expression in order to connect with your soul. The creator creates. The spark of the divine creator that lives in you also creates. Ergo, you can access both through creating — whatever form your creativity takes.

This is the longest of all of the steps, and so it has the longest chapter. Why? Well, if we follow Einstein's advice — and by all accounts he was a pretty bright guy, so I'll follow him — we should spend the bulk of our time exploring the problem. Do you want the good news or the bad news first? Well, the bad news is: You're the problem. The good news is: You're the solution. So if you explore you, you're addressing both the problem and the solution. Brilliant!

How do you understand the problem? In the introduction, I talked about the problem being the fact that something woke you up, and there's this really annoying earworm of discontent in your head that is telling you that you haven't lived up to your potential and it might be too late and even if it isn't too late you don't know what to do or how to even get started.

Let's dig down another layer and spend some more time on describing the problem. I'm going to add some assumptions I've made about you — based solely on the fact that they were true for me at one time.

- You don't know or can't remember who you really are.

- You've grown apart (from your true, inner or higher self).

- You don't know what you want, what you like or even what you enjoy.

- Your beliefs (mostly about yourself) haven't been updated in a while.

- You might need a little healing.

- You need a (fill in the blank) makeover.

- You've forgotten your super powers.

- You don't trust yourself or your judgment.

Any of these ring true? Did you check your gut? Did you maybe tear up a little about thinking that some of these things might be true for you? If yes, good for you! Truth-finder operating within acceptable parameters!

Now what? Oh, this part is work, but it's also fun. I want you get to know yourself. Really know yourself — your mind, body, heart, spirit and soul. I want you to spend time finding out what you think, what you like, what you feel, what you believe, what you're good at, what you make, how you create and how you express yourself.

My editor, Kate, suggested that I might want to make this whole *getting to know yourself* bit a little more enticing. I guess I'm looking at it from the other side — having done it and enjoyed it and found it to be one of the best things I've ever done. But once I've told you about it, you might think it doesn't sound like all that fun. After all, you're a little bit disgusted and disappointed with yourself, right? I could ask you to just trust me and give it a try. But I'll listen to Kate and make it more enticing.

The bottom line is that you are stuck with yourself, so you might as well make the best of it and get to work liking yourself. Wait, that's not very enticing, is it? I'll try again.

1. You already have at least three of the most important criteria for lifelong best friend status, according to my collection of refrigerator magnets:

2. You get all your own jokes.

3. You know so many of your own secrets you could blackmail yourself.

You've seen yourself at your worst and you're still here.

That's already a pretty good foundation for a friendship, but there really is more. Remember when you were younger (say high school or college) and you had lots of time to hang out with new people? Do you remember how interesting, how energizing it was to ask them all kinds of questions and get to know them? Maybe it was a little scary, too, because what if they didn't like you? But remember how much straight-up fun it was to try things they liked that you might not have done before? That's how you built friendships, right? You found out about them and you did stuff together, including new stuff. And your connection got deeper when you went through stuff together.

Can you remember what that felt like? When everything in life seemed to have that new car smell? That's the feeling we're going for here! But the *really* good news is that you don't have to start over. When you reach out to connect with yourself, you are really reconnecting with a dear friend — a little time has gone by, you're a bit out of touch, but there's still a lot of good history here. As you get to know yourself again, you get to reconnect with themes, plots, sub-plots, major and minor characters from your past. You get to choose which ones to keep, which ones to archive and which ones to pull out and resuscitate or completely reinvent.

It's scary to look in the mirror, I know. It gets easier with practice, and you can think of it as pursuing fun — kind of like having a play date with yourself. This change thing doesn't always have to be all dark and introspective, chasing flaws and monsters.

I have to confess that I'm feeling just a little proud of myself for not going for the "You're worth it!" or "Be your own best friend!" moment so blatantly that I made myself puke.

When I started on my J-O-U-R-N-E-Y of self-discovery, I ran into something called Aura-Soma. I didn't really know what it was, but someone I really trusted recommended it. They told me it was the best thing ever, but they couldn't really describe it. So I just went with it.

I went to Elizabeth's house with a group of friends. Elizabeth is this tall, beautiful woman with gorgeously wild, curly hair. She has a personality and a heart as big as the sky. Elizabeth is many things, including an intuitive and an Aura-Soma practitioner. She told us that we were going to do a consult, but we would start with a guided meditation. We did, which was totally amazing, but not on topic, so I'm moving on.

When we got to the consult, she showed us a cabinet of beautiful bottles. I later learned that the bottles are made of up both an oil-based and a water-based faction, with the oil floating in the top half of the bottle on top of the water. So each bottle can have two different colors in it. Each bottle shines like jewels. So pretty.

When it came time for my consult, she had me choose four bottles. Her instructions were to choose the bottles using my intuition, based on which ones shone or sang out to me, and to pay attention to the order in which I chose them.

I picked my four bottles, and what I learned was truly life changing. There is a universal language of color, and there are cultural and personal meanings that each of us overlay on top of the universal meanings. As Elizabeth and I explored each bottle, the choice-position it was in, the messages of colors in the top factions and the bottom factions, something really big shifted for me. I understood things about myself that I really hadn't understood before, much less believed. As I decided to take a bottle and work with it, Elizabeth told me, "You are the colors you choose."

I worked with the bottle and I had profound experiences, mostly learning about myself and about my talents. I went back a couple of months later to do another consult. Again, when I saw the bottles, my breath was taken away by how beautiful they were. I know I sound like a real zealot here, but it's absolutely true. That's how I felt. I'm struggling to find words that mean "amazing" but don't make me sound like somebody on *The Bachelor*. Anyway, as I gushed about how beautiful the bottles were, Elizabeth again said, "You are the colors you choose."

I had another *amazing* (sic) consult and took a bottle home to work with, and again I had a huge personal growth spurt.

The third time I went back... same story. Fast forward to Elizabeth saying, again, "You are the colors you choose," and I finally got it. *The bottles are so beautiful. I am the colors I choose. I am beautiful.* For a smart girl, I felt really slow. I learned a whole lot more from Aura-Soma and from Elizabeth. But really, truly coming to know and believe that I was beautiful — that I had a beautiful soul and it could be seen — was such a profound change for me. I felt like I was introduced to the real me for the first time. It also profoundly changed the way I "worked on" myself. I no longer approached it as a huge to-do list of DIY projects, things to fix. I started believing in the things I was good at, my own special gifts and talents, and they really lined up with the things I loved. I crowded out the things I didn't want anymore by adding in more of the things I did want.

What's the moral of the story here? When you want to find out more about yourself, when you want to really get to know who you are, be very open to new ways. Explore the non-traditional, the alternative, the woo-woo things that come across your path — and they *will* cross your path! Check out whatever seems shiny and interesting. Yes, it is officially research, and you get credit for skipping ahead to Step R, you overachiever you! Think of it as trying out a different lens, and you just might see a totally different side of yourself. You might use this new lens to see the world, other people and how we all relate to each other differently. And if you can seek out an Aura-Soma consult, DO IT!!!!! By the way, I was so changed by my Aura-Soma journey that I became an Aura-Soma practitioner — I practice what I preach. (My niece would put an *LOL* here.)

EXERCISES:

Here are some exercises for really getting to know yourself again. I hope you are enticed to try them!

1. Interview yourself or get someone you trust to interview you. Make sure to ask questions that cover all five aspects: mind, body, heart, spirit, soul. Write down the answers in your journal. Be sure to capture any insights on your blank cards. In my program, I interview the client, and it takes almost two hours. You can download the list of interview questions from the website. TIP: Pretend (if you must) that the interviewer is interviewing someone famous and very, very interesting!

2. Take a bunch of online personality quizzes, like Myers-Briggs, Strength Finder, IQ tests, the innumerable Facebook quizzes ("What kind of mythical character are you?" "Which Disney dwarf are you?" etc.)

3. Explore numerology or astrology. Get a psychic reading.

4. Get an Aura-Soma consultation. Oh I so highly recommend this! Check out my website www.tapasforyoursoul.com/aura-soma/ for more info on Aura-Soma and how to get a consultation.)

5. Look at old pictures, scrapbooks, art, accomplishments, letters, transcripts, etc. Remember. Interview your parents, siblings, friends or grandparents. Ask them questions like, "What do you like about me?" "What was I like as a child?" "What do you think I'm good at?" Be really open to hearing the good stuff. Remember, the goal here is to get back in touch with your potential, so, by definition, that's gonna be good stuff. The goal is not to open up old wounds or find faults.

6. Write in your journal. Observe how you spend your time, what you think, how you feel. Gather information and insights.

7. Track the physical stuff — what you eat, drink, how you move, how you feel, how you sleep — all that stuff — in rigorous detail. (You can get tracking sheets from my website.)

8. Do a health history with a health coach. This is usually offered for free and it can tell you a lot about your health.

Remember to write down on your blank cards any truths or insights you discover.

In my 12-week transformation program, we spend almost half of the time on activities of self-discovery, exploration, data gathering and evaluation. It really is the biggest chunk of work. And every one of my clients has been totally delighted with the person they've discovered by going through this part of the journey.

In my program, every week we create a tasting menu (hence the program name's tapas reference) made up of tiny activities to do to track, discover, explore, sample, research and experience each of the five aspects of the self: mind, body, heart, spirit and soul. You can go to my website to get a sample menu for each step of the journey, and see more of the exercises we use in the longer version of the program. If you're already interested in checking out the Tapas For Your Soul program, or if you become interested further along in the program, you can schedule a call with me to find out more, at www.Talk toMaggie.com.

Summing it all up:

As you get to know yourself better on this first step of the journey, I hope you discover some things like these:

• You are just divine, baby, and don't you forget it.

• You are complex and beautiful.

• You have a gorgeous mind.

• You have a miraculous body, but you are more than just your body.

• Your heart is full of wonderful emotions, and the more you explore, the more you feel.

• Your beliefs are probably a little out of date, and you're going to need to revisit them, but there are some things that are really important to you, and they remain true.

• You are truly creative, and you're pretty interested in getting back in touch with some things you used to love to do.

Here's a free bonus: a quick hit for each category, guaranteed to make you feel a whole bunch better really quickly:

Mind: Follow a Google trail about something that interests you.

Body: Drink more water and stretch every day.

Heart: Make a gratitude list.

Spirit: Find a song or piece of music that makes your gut feel good.

Soul: Doodle (in meetings, on conference calls, while waiting for the dentist).

What do you think about the concept that you are a spiritual being having a physical life? Is it new to you? Does it change the way you think at all? How?

*What wonderful things have you discovered
about yourself? What did you remember?
What treasures did the interview uncover?*

MIND: What thoughts, insights discoveries do you have?
What are you really interested in?
What are you curious about? Do you follow up?

BODY: What thoughts, insights discoveries do you have? What did you discover from the physical tracking sheets? Any patterns that you hadn't seen before?

HEART: What thoughts, insights discoveries do you have? What kinds of relationships and feelings do you have? Are you generally happy? Loving? Grateful? Or...?

SPIRIT: What thoughts, insights discoveries do you have? What do you believe? What do you believe about yourself? About your place in the world? What you can and can't do? How's your trust level? What do you practice?

SOUL: What thoughts, insights discoveries do you have?
How do you see the divine reflected in you?
How do you create your world? How are you creative?

Trigger words: Trust, love, clarity, genius, ability, talent, health, illness, graceful, flexible, strength, love, lonely, giving, approval, capable, worth, deserve, earn, safe, art, beauty, creative, eternal, divine, spark

Chapter 4.

O — Okay, Who Do You Want to Be?

"A man cannot be comfortable without his own approval."

~ Mark Twain (*Let's just pretend he said, "person," okay?*)

You've just figured out who you are. The next step of the journey is to find out who you want to be. Spoiler alert: This might not be as dramatic a change as you've been thinking it would be. Or, guess what? It might be bigger, way bigger. But, chances are, since you now know yourself a whole lot better, who you want to be will be a better fit than the original picture you had of yourself when you started — *that* potential you was probably still wearing oversized shoulder pads and mighty big hair. Just sayin'.

Key Concepts

How are you going to find out what you want? Shouldn't you know already? Well, yes, you probably do have a pretty good idea. But you might not be listening to the right inner sources. In Chapter 2, you tried using your gut or intuition as a barometer of truth, and I said that later we would explore some additional options. Well, it's now later. So here are some additional indicators pointing to the right inner sources at your disposal: emotions (especially fear and love), dreams, flow, synchronicity, signs and divination.

Emotions. Emotions are the experience of a state of consciousness, as distinguished from cognitive and volitional states. Emotions and desires are powerful informational messages from our inner guidance systems to our conscious mind. Blah, blah, blah — but true. That all means that you *feel* emotions, you don't *think* emotions. When you feel emotions, the experience goes to your mind to be translated so your mind can tell you what it means. You engage both the heart and the mind.

Fear. Fear is a vital response to danger — whether the danger is real or imaginary. For most people, fear is unpleasant, and we tend to think of it as something bad that we need to eradicate or overcome. But you can't brute force your way out of fear. So let's try to reframe fear as something we can use. Fear evolved as a tool to help us survive. Let's evolve it further to help us thrive. Fear indicates that you care deeply about something — so look inside to see what's so important to you. Fear might indicate that you have some information that says something you care about may be in danger. Ask yourself what that information might be and what you can do about it. Fear might really be nervousness about stepping out of your comfort zone. In any case, try stepping back from the emotional impact of fear. Go to a place of curiosity where you can say, "Isn't that interesting. I'm afraid of yoghurt. What could that be telling me?" Treat yourself with compassion and understanding, and use the information for your highest good.

Love. This just might appear to be the most obvious indicator. We're all familiar with the "lovely" descriptions of love: Love is patient, kind, doesn't envy nor boast... etc. Love conquers all. All true, no doubt. Sometimes. For some people. But love just isn't always that simple or pure. It's really complex. Love is also fierce and protective and hard and tough. You can love people, places, things, ideas, art and more. Romantic love can be accompanied by selfishness or insecurity or jealousy. You can be very impatient with someone you love. Love alone doesn't conquer *everything*. Love has so many facets. At least for this journey, let's take the view that love is very personal to you, and who you love or what kind of love you feel tells you something important. You have to be the one to decipher what that message is.

Dreams. Your dreams are *you* telling yourself important things. Your dreams can be downloads from spirit or your higher self. They can be from your subconscious mind, working through a problem, giving you a warning, processing events. You are the best one to understand the meaning of your dreams.

Flow and ease. Think of life as a river. There is energy in the river as it flows toward its destination. Think of yourself as a swimmer in the river. You can swim upstream, against the flow, and expend a lot of energy. Maybe you'll make some progress, but if you stop for one moment, the flow will carry you away. If you turn around, you can float and use the energy of the current to carry you. If you swim with the flow, you feel incredible power. We've been conditioned to believe that we need to overcome obstacles and swim upstream. We learned it from concepts we hear — like, "No pain no gain," "Nothing good comes without a struggle" and "Adversity builds character." But the truth is, we don't have to believe that. You can choose to know that life is just better if you actively go with the flow. It's your river! Consider feeling at ease to be indicator that you are following the right path for you.

Signs and synchronicity. When we do stop struggling and start working *with* the flow, a remarkable thing happens. We start to become aware of an increasing number of seemingly coincidental things that are in our paths. These can be opportunities, insights, reinforcing signs — all manner of synchronistic jewels. The magic is that they have been there all along, but we have spent so much of our energy and focus on the struggle that we had no room to see them. Signs tend to show up repeatedly, until we get it through our thick skulls that they *are* signs. Signs and synchronicity are indicators that we are going with the flow of *our own* river.

Divination. Divination is a way to connect to your intuition. The mainstream understanding is that divination is trying to predict the future. Balderdash. Divination is really a way of connecting to your intuition to see and understand the truth; to tap into your inner system to guide you to appropriate action, wisdom and peace of mind. See the exercises below to use your body as a source of divination.

So now that I've introduced these concepts, what do you do with them? You use them, silly! Yes, I'll tell you how, and you'll get exercises to help you practice.

But, in case you're at all resistant, let me try to talk you into it.

Say you need to make a recommendation to your boss about one software package over another. You wouldn't just go to the software vendor's website to get a summary of features and make a decision on what you're going to recommend, would you? I sure hope not. (The software vendors hope you would, you know.) You'd probably read some reviews, maybe look for some customer references and maybe get access to a trial period so you could check out the look and feel and usability of the software before you recommended buying it. You'd also probably consider how difficult it is to learn, how compatible it is with other programs and yada yada. In other words, you'd use as many reliable sources of information as you could get, and *then* you'd decide what to recommend.

Well, I'm saying that you have all of these additional reliable sources of information, so don't you want to use them? And here's the deal — these sources are all coming from and vetted by you. What's bringing these sources into your awareness is the *you* that has your own best interests at heart, and whose judgment you are (finally) coming to trust again. Convinced? Why don't you take the idea out for a test drive.

Oh, but before you do, there's one more thing I'd like you to think about: fear vs. love. Often, we make our choices from one of those two places — fear or love. As I said above, there are times when fear is informative and helpful. Fear is all about reacting to a threat — real or imagined — and about self-preservation. Preservation can be disguised as practicality and security. That's not about growth or inspiration or happiness. When you come from a place of fear, you are giving away your power — and you really aren't *choosing* anything. It takes awareness and some courage to step into your power and choose from a place of love. But the payoff is huge. (CliffsNotes: fear can be a source of information, but love is the deciding factor.)

EXERCISES:

Play with trusting your emotions as guidance for your mind to do some investigation. Pay attention to all the things that make you feel good, make you smile or make you happy. Use your mind to discover what you like about them and how you can get more of it into your life. That's what you want, right?

Interpret your dreams, and look for messages. While you can go to numerous books and websites to get information on the meanings of your dreams, you are actually completely equipped to decode your dreams by yourself. The simplest way is to write down the key elements of the dream (*not* the gory details). With the understanding that the purpose of the dream is to tell you something meaningful about your life now, use your intuition to translate each element into a message. Seriously, the first thing that comes into your head is probably correct. Once you have the series of messages, you can get the overall theme of the dream. Once you've practiced doing this a few times and feel comfortable that you understand what your dreams are telling you, try setting a dream intention before you go to sleep. Ask yourself questions like, "What do I need to know?" or "What's next?"

Take a synchronicity wander. Pick a place to start, somewhere that is connected to what's on your mind or in your heart, and follow the trail of signs that will appear. This works best in an urban area or in nature, but not so well in a suburban area. No, I don't know why.

Use divination to learn more about what you want or what you think might be good for you. For example, when choosing between meal options, use your body to judge whether something is right for you by seeing whether an option feels heavy or light. Or, hold an item in your hand and use your body as a pendulum — do you lean forward (yes) or back away (no) from the item? If you want to try something adventurous, use a real pendulum to see what your intuition is telling you. You're holding it in your hand, so it's connected to you and your intuition.

Tap into your soul by creating a vision board/collage, painting or drawing. You'll discover that you are attracted to certain colors, words and images and that they evoke a spark of desire that maybe wasn't yet on your radar.

Remember to write down on your blank cards any truth or insight you discover.

We've all heard about amazing stories of intuition, right? Well I have a story about intuition that literally saved my life.

When I was in college, I had a really cute, bronze, vintage '65 Mustang convertible. That has nothing to do with the story, but I still love that car. In my sophomore year, I was driving back to school from spring break. I had to drive on Highway 12, between Fairfield and Lodi in the central valley of California. It was — and still is –a pretty danger-ous road. Back in the day, it was a two-lane highway, with no center divider, out in the boondocks, with lots of wild-life all around, and the highway itself was a levee in many places, with water on either side. It was getting close to dusk and I was driving along, probably singing loudly to an Eagles song or something. All of a sudden, my stom-ach dropped, and I thought, "Oh, this road is danger-ous. What if a rabbit or some other animal were to run out in the road?" My brain answered, "Well, you'd slow down and swerve so you don't hit it, of course." My gut came back with "No, a truck might be coming, and I'd get hit head-on." My brain got working on that scenario. I couldn't swerve to the right because I'd go off into the water. I couldn't swerve to the left because I'd get hit by the truck. I couldn't slam on the brakes because I might lose control, swerve to either side, or someone could be on my tail and hit me from behind. Okay, nothing else to do but hit the rabbit.

Seriously, less than a minute later, that exact scenario happened, with rabbit, oncoming truck and tailgating car. I hit the rabbit. I felt really bad, of course. I also knew that before getting and processing the intuition, my instinct would have been to slam on the brakes. I believe that intuition saved my life. Poor rabbit. :-(

Probably, my brain took in all kinds of information that influenced that scenario — there were probably skid marks and rabbit road kill that I saw without consciously noticing. But why did I choose that exact time to run through the possible scenarios? I don't have to under-stand intuition to trust it. Since that day, I've intentionally gone with my gut whenever I can. I use intuition to make all kinds of choices, or at least to help me understand which way I'm leaning. If I'm torn between options, I let my intuition be my deciding factor. I've used intuition in business consistently. I consider intuition a distinct advan-tage in the competitive sport of executive management. It's so rarely wrong that I now only keep track of the times that I *didn't* go with my gut, but should have!

Now that you've done the exercises above, the real assignment for this chapter is to use your journal to describe who you want to be and what you want for yourself. You have a few more tools in your belt to help you discern your own personal truth. If you get stuck, use the jump lines below to jump into writing. Set a timer for 10 minutes and write to finish these lines:

What I want you to know…

What I really want to write about…

What makes me happy…

What I want more of…

If I had a magic wand…

Or, use any other jump line that gets you started to write about your new picture of what you want.

Go to my website for vision board instructions and additional resources for this step at www.WhoopsIforgotmy potential.com.

Summing it all up:

What I want for you is:

- Be comfortable using different ways besides your analytical brain to find out what you want.

- Don't just be afraid of fear, use it to teach you what you value.

- Pay attention to what your dreams and other signs are telling you.

- Allow room for the idea that you don't need to struggle for everything, and that ease can be an indicator that you're becoming aligned with your true self.

- Cultivate a growing sense, maybe even a vision, of what you want to be, how you want to feel and some things you might want to do.

FIELD NOTES

What have you believed about struggle?
Have there been any sayings that have shaped your
thoughts (like "no pain, no gain")?

✍ FIELD NOTES ✍

How do you react to the ideas of ease, flow, signs and synchronicity?

Explore a dream or a strong emotion or strong, unexpected reaction — what are you trying to tell yourself?

Do you have any intuition stories? A time when you went against what your gut was telling you? When you followed your intuition? When you knew what was going to happen before it did? What happened?

Chapter 5.

U — Understand the Gap

"Honesty is the first chapter in the book of wisdom."

~ Thomas Jefferson

So now you know who you are. You have some ideas about what you want and who you want to be. And, by the way, it's okay if you don't want to change much, but just want to add in more things that make you happy. It's also totally okay to want to make big changes. You really can't get this part wrong, because, as you now know, the earworm of discontent will wake you up if you need to make more changes. Life is an iterative process.

This step of the journey is about understanding the gap between who you are and what you want to be. In business transformation projects, this step is called "Gap Analysis." It's when you look at the Current State and the Ideal (or Future) State and figure out what you need to fix or do to build a bridge to get from here to there. "Gap analysis" is a good name for this step, because you are going to do some analysis. But you're going to go a bit deeper, because you want to use the analysis to get to the insights, right? Information without insights is just random data neatly organized. You can quote me on that, but if you do, please say it in a very authoritative voice so that people think you are an expert.

Let me tell you right now, this could be the most tedious of all the steps. And it can be a bit challenging and confusing. It is not a crystal clear or cut and dried step. Here's why: The more you focus in on what is true for you, the more you will go back and update what you know about yourself and what you want to be and do. You might go back and forth between the current you and the ideal you, and you will definitely add things to the who-you-want-to-be pile. You might take some things off that pile, too. You'll discover that some of the things that you thought were true just aren't anymore. That's okay. Really. This means you are getting better and better at this self-discovery process.

As I edit this, I feel compelled to recommend that you go back and watch the movie *Back to the Future*. This step is kinda like that. Watching that movie won't help clarify anything here, but it is fun.

Key Concepts

Objectivity. Oh my god. I went to look for an easy definition of objectivity, and it's just crazy. There's the philosophical point of view, the central philosophical concept, the idea as opposed to subjectivity… ugh. Just *ugh*. I wanted something simple for a definition and was taken back to tortured freshman philosophy discussions. Sorry, you didn't need to know all that, did you? Here's what I mean by being objective: staying as clear of your prejudices, biases, emotional reactions and fears as you possibly can.

Perspective is maintaining a consistent point of view that, in this case, is taken from a point outside of the landscape. Perspective gives you a frame of reference.

Scientist's hat. Well, it's not as cool as an archeologist's hat, but it's not as dorky as a math hat. You will need to put it on, though. The scientist's hat does have a cool feature that makes you look at things through the eyes of many different disciplines — archeology, sociology, psychology, physiology and nutrition, to name a few. You won't become a nerdy expert in each field, but you will gain the ability to see patterns and develop enough of a critical eye to discern what's important. Definitely close enough for jazz (which is not really a science).

Self-observation is pretty close to a super power in this step. You want to be able to separate yourself from your situation enough to observe and gather data without getting so caught up in the situation that you can't trust your reactions. You've got to be able to put on your cool hat, remember?

Okay, so back to the job of understanding the gap between who you are and who you want to be. I'll get around to talking about a structure for understanding the gaps in a minute.

Before I do that, I want to give you a really big warning: *do not judge*! The #1 mistake people make is that they don't like the gap, so they judge it. They think the gap is bad, they see nothing but flaws in themselves, they feel guilt and shame. So if you see yourself start to do that... stop right away. Step away from the gap and go put your cool science hat back on — because it must have fallen off, right? Really, don't judge the gap. Or yourself. Come on, give yourself a break. Judging yourself in this step is like thinking your puppy is bad because he doesn't know how to sit before you take him to obedience class. He's not bad. Take him to class and he'll be fine!

Maybe you don't like the gap. That's fine. It still doesn't mean you get to judge it. That will totally get in the way of finding the best way to bridge the gap. So just observe, okay? Did I say that enough times? Oooh. I just thought of something (this is a "duh"). We wanna bridge the gap, right. What's that mean? We use a bridge to *get over it*!

Get over the fact that there is a gap. Translation: You are not who you want to be because there is a big "yet" there. I like a big "yet" way better than a big "but." (Hee, hee. She said, "butt." Sorry, sorry, sorry. But I'm still laughing. Out loud.)

I know that not judging the gap sounds a whole lot easier than it is. Not judging is almost the same as acceptance, and we all know that ain't easy. So, what do I have for you that might make it easier? One thing is perspective. If you don't pick the right perspective, you're going to take sides or switch back and forth, and that's just not going to be pretty. Have you ever taken a drawing class? I did and, honestly, perspective was one of the toughest concepts for me to grasp. My chairs and tables always looked like they were in different rooms. Like I said, not pretty.

I know you well enough by now that I know you aren't gonna make it easy on yourself. So, here, let me help. Pick a point to view from that is a little bit above it all. No, not in a snooty way, in a bird's-eye-view kind of way. That's a nice, objective, view that will actually show you the shortest way between two points. And you won't need to get all judgy or defensive.

One more thing. No matter how objective you try to be, this part might be kind of hard or scary or overwhelming. In the preparation chapter, I told you that you might need some tools to help you handle things. Well, here's where you might need them. If you have tools that work for you (things like yoga or breathing or meditation or tapping). Great, smoke 'em if you got 'em. Working with a coach can save you a lot of trouble. If you don't have tools or a coach, check out the tapas menu on my website supporting this chapter: www.Whoopslforgotmypotential.com. If you want to talk to me about working with me, you can schedule a call to find out more, at www.TalktoMaggie.com.

Okay, just one more thing before we talk about how to analyze the gap, and that's a word on healing. I'm going to get quite serious for a minute. As you observe yourself, you might notice some things that need healing. We all have an amazing capacity to heal — emotionally, mentally, physically and spiritually — but we have to allow ourselves the time and support to let our natural processes work. If you find something big that needs to be healed and don't feel equipped to handle it yourself, get help. Don't waste time making a decision, just go ahead and get help — because you deserve to heal, and you deserve help. You are important and worth it. And you might not be able to make any more progress toward achieving your potential until you do. Okay?

Now, if you are just mildly f'd up like all the rest of us, you can choose a new technology for healing. The old technology has been used in talk therapy for years. It involves remembering, reliving and processing traumatic events. It is very time consuming, and often prolongs the feelings and pain. New thinking shows that by reliving and remembering, we actually more firmly embed the trauma by writing it into our short-term memory. Here's some good news: there is a new technology that is based on releasing and relieving, not reliving. By releasing, we activate our personal power of choice and actively let go of the hold that the trauma has had on us. The act of observing puts us in a great position to recognize and release.

There are some wonderful options for releasing therapies for healing. I'll mention just a few here, but you can research others that might interest you. In fact, researching (aka trying them out) can be an exercise for you in the next chapter. Generally, they fall in three categories: energy work, body work and mind-body work.

First on my list is Aura-Soma (a combination of all three categories) which is a beautiful way to recognize, understand and release on a cellular level without reliving on an intellectual level.

In the **body work** category, there are several options. Massage, which releases the memories that we store in our body, whether bona fide trauma or (just) the crippling bullshit beliefs we have about ourselves. Another is Tension, Stress and Trauma Release (TRE), a set of exercises for releasing tension and trauma (Google it for more info). Other body work modalities include cranio-sacral therapy, shiatsu, and breath work. There are lots more of these to explore.

Energy therapies can include Reiki, Jin Shin Jyitsu, healing touch and even prayer.

Mind-body work can include meditation, visualization, hypnosis and intention.

Exploring these options is really a twofer. You get the benefit of releasing things that need to be released (not re-lived) *and* you get to practice sampling and experiencing things to see what you like. That's one of the most important skills to take with you on this journey!

Working with a coach can be an awesome accelerant for discovery and for healing. Coaches can work hand-in-hand or side-by-side with whatever else you have going on. A coaching program can be the catalyst that helps you discover how to bridge the gap. It's really, really important to pick the right coach. How do you know who is right for you? Interview them! Treat it like a first date and ask questions that tell you whether or not this relationship can go anywhere. Do you like them? Do you have any kind of chemistry? How do their values line up with yours? Do you feel like you can trust them? Are they as smart as you are? Trust your gut. I guarantee that any coach worth their salt is going to be choosy about who their clients are, too. It has to be a good match. I've worked with amazing coaches and I've worked with mediocre coaches. I've gotten something out of working with both, but when there is really a fit — when *I* think that they are amazing — the difference for me has been astronomical, even life-changing. That's how it's supposed to be, right? So be choosy!

Alrighty then, we can move on now.

Just how do you go about analyzing the gap? If you are the kind of person who knows how to do this, or you think you can wing it, go for it. If you'd like a structure, because you feel a little lost, go on over to my website www.WhoopsIforgotmypotential.com and download a worksheet.

Basically, you use what you've generated so far (journals, tracking sheets, vision board, etc.) to identify things that seem like important ways to bridge the gap between who you are now and what you want to be. Categorize them as *mind, body, heart, spirit and soul*. Spend a little extra time on the physical tracking sheets, because you can sometimes see patterns there that you couldn't see before. Pick the biggest, juiciest, most important ones. Put the rest in your *maybe later* file.

Take another pass through the list and see if there is anything that really is more of a quick hit. In a transformation project, a quick hit is something that you can pretty much just do. You don't need permission do to it, it doesn't cost much money or take much planning or effort, and there's not much risk that it will cause any unintended consequences. So if you find a quick hit, take it off the list. You can choose how and when to address it, but it doesn't need to be on the list. Just do it.

Is there anything that needs healing? Think about what I said about healing earlier. If you need serious help, get it. If not, make a *needs healing* category. And that's it. Now you have your research list for the next step. And if you maintained your objectivity and you didn't beat yourself up or judge, I am so proud of you!

Here's my story on the value of tracking and analyzing and objectivity. Pretty much every diet coach in the world tells you to keep a food and exercise journal and says that will shine the light on all of your habits and help you stay accountable. Been there, done that a bunch of times, and yes, it does work. But, last year, I decided to become a certified health coach. As I did, I really learned about the dangers of hidden sugars. Don't worry, this isn't gonna be a sugar story. I started a program to give up sugar. In the program, you write down everything you eat *and* how it makes you feel. I'd never done that before, but okay. I wrote down the normal stomach cramps and gas and stuff. Then you eliminate things with "hidden" sugars and observe how you feel. Pretty damn good. No stomach cramps or gas. And I feel lighter and have more energy. Okay, now you start adding things back one at a time. Well, I was a bread-aholic, so that was pretty much the first thing I added back. OMG. That hurts. *And I used to think that feeling was normal?* What the hell? Shortcut to the end... I have a gluten sensitivity, and I never knew it until I set up a controlled experiment and observed. Of course, I doubted the results and tested it again. But I got the same results. No judgment. Knowledge. Now I can choose whether or not to eat bread, because I know the consequences.

The lesson: Go ahead and gather some data and analyze it. You just might learn something unexpected and very, very valuable.

Remember to write down on your blank cards any truth or insight you discover.

Summing it all up:

- Science hats are cooler than math hats, but not as cool as Indiana Jones' archeologist's hat.

- The step of understanding the gap takes a lot of set-up, because we usually go to a place of shame or frustration about the things on the list.

- I would love for you to be able to look objectively at what makes up the gap between who you are now and who you want to be, without judging or feeling shame.

- If you have things that need healing, seek health. And I would really love for you to be open to trying alternative methods of healing that allow for release and relief, not reliving.

- I want you to get excited about having a list of things that might work to bridge the gap, because that's what you'll use to explore and do research. And that's the *really* fun part!!

And now, let's go have some fun.

≈ FIELD NOTES ≈

No judging allowed: If you start to judge either gaps or bridges, stop, take a breath, put on a cool hat and observe. Why are you judging, and what does that tell you? Where are you prone to judge? Why do you think that is?

FIELD NOTES

Identify some of the gaps you see.

Brainstorm ways you might want to bridge the gaps.

Do you have any healing or releasing to do? Are you interested in exploring some new healing modalities? If you try them, write about the experience.

📖✍ Field Notes ✍📖

---

*Trigger words: curious, observe, remark, notice,
lack, need, skill set, training, barrier, hard, remove,
perspective, guilty, should, embarrass, shame, chasm,
excuses, defensive, release, heal, recover, admit, forgive,
dream, achieve, future, possible, transform, bridge,
envision, transition, unlimited, uncluttered,
unfettered, free, courage*

Chapter 6.

R — Research Your Options

"Act and behave as though you are the person you
 want to be."

~ Bernie Siegel, MD

Here's where you thank the earworm, because now you
get to play! I hope you thought that getting to know yourself again and dreaming about what you want to be, do
and feel was fun. Even if you only secretly thought it was
fun. You're a fun person, right? You'd better think so. Like I
said before, at least you get all your own jokes. This step in
the journey — research — is where the serious fun (oxymo-
ron?) begins. This is where you get to go off and explore
anything your heart desires — and call it research!

Key Concepts

Pick the right thing for you. The #1 reason most people
fail at making a big life change isn't because they can't do
it or because they are scared or they aren't smart enough
or any of the other reasons your analytical brain would
think. The real reason is that they pick the wrong thing to

change. They don't really take the time to pick the right thing *for them*. They listen to what some "expert" tells them they *should* do and, of course, if it doesn't really fit them, it's not gonna stick.

Stopping isn't failing. The #2 reason most people fail at something is because they call it failing. Actually, it wasn't failure but a learning experience, and they discovered that something wasn't a fit for them — so it was a successful learning experience. Instead of saying, "Well, I tried that. It's not for me, thank you very much," they say that they failed.

One size does not fit all. Don't buy into that myth. Sometimes one size fits most, but even then there are some wonderful people who don't fall into that "most" category. I'm 5'12". I never fit into the "all" category, and rarely into the "most," and I don't even fit into the "never" category.

You are unique — magically, mysteriously unique - and you are constantly evolving into the newest version of you. And it's not just you that's unique, right? Every snowflake is different; no two leaves are the same: similar, sure but not identical. Diversity is the biggest blessing of our existence.

You can try anything for a week. This is one of the basic foundations of my Tapas program, and I'd like you to use it in your research. You don't have to commit to anything for the rest of your life — just give it a try for a week. Let go of your preconceived ideas and be open to trying everything with an open mind. Seriously, how do you know you don't like asparagus if you haven't tried it since you were five? Maybe your tastes have changed. Maybe not — but you can always spit it out, right? Then you will really know you don't like it. Or maybe you do like it, and a whole new wonderful world of green things opens up before you in a panoramic vista!

Everybody has one interesting thing to say to you. Some have more. You can even learn something from a complete idiot — even if what you learn is "Wow, I really don't believe what that idiot said. I need to stay away from him." Or maybe someone hands you a tiny piece of a puzzle that helps you make sense of something else. If you keep an open mind, always looking for that one thing they have for you, you'll discover a web of interconnectedness and synchronicity. It's really, really cool, and it feels like cheating, because things start to come so easily.

You don't have to commit before you try; try before you commit. That's probably pretty obvious to you by now, but even the obvious is worth mentioning occasionally!

This step is about researching your options. You are going to take the list of things you identified in the previous step as gaps that need to be bridged, and turn it into a list of things to research. You'll choose what you want to do in the next step. Right now, you are just exploring and discovering and trying and tasting and experimenting. I call this "living life on Google." If something piques your interest, go check it out. Follow the trail. Rev up that search engine.

If there's a problem with this approach, it really comes in when we commit to something and decide that it really is for us, before we try it. This applies to big things (like relationships), medium-sized things (like diets or food plans), and even small things. Here's a great example of a small thing. I have this annoying habit of going into a store, trying on big girl shoes — the kinds of shoes I *should* wear if I'm going to dress for success. They really aren't exactly comfy, but they don't hurt too much (in the store). So I buy them. The first time I really wear them, my feet hurt so much that I can't think of anything else. I take them off and walk around the office barefoot — which is so not the dress for success look. And another pair of expensive shoes sits at the bottom of my closet. Wash, rinse and repeat about every three months, and I've got a whole pile of really nice shoes to take to the women's shelter. (The best part of quitting my corporate job was getting to wear Fitflops or Hoka One Ones almost every day, all year round.)

You can extrapolate this story to fit almost anything. Check out the list of things you think you've failed at. Relationships? Jobs? Diet and exercise? Hobbies? Finding a church home? Finding your tribe? Now please stand on your head and look at it differently. You are succeeding at researching your options. You are checking stuff out, trying before you buy, really kicking the tires.

Enter the Tapas Menu. Do you know about tapas? Tapas are small, sample-sized servings of food. In a tapas bar, there's a menu full of a wide variety of tapas dishes. You put together your meal by ordering a customized choice of samples to try. The serving of tapas is designed to encourage conversation, because people are not so focused on eating an entire meal, but instead on exploring the menu. It's a really fun way to have a meal with friends — kind of like eating by just ordering appetizers, but with a lot more variety. From the first chapter of this book, I've encouraged you to try different things to find out how you think and feel about them. Now you get to amp it up a bit.

I want you to turn your list into a tapas menu. You don't have to try everything on the menu, but you have to pick a lot of stuff. And you definitely have to pick at least one thing from each category (mind, body, heart, spirit, soul). As you do this, something magical will happen. Your taste buds for life will come alive again. You'll add more and more things to the list. You'll get excited. No more waking up in the middle of the night with the earworm of discontent squawking at you. Instead, you'll bolt up thinking, "Oh, I should try making kites out of my old t-shirt collection!" or "I remember that really interesting girl from Auckland. I wonder what she's doing now. Maybe I should check out New Zealand" or "I know what my tattoo should be!" or "How did the theme song from *SG-1* go?" It can all seem very random, but it's your creative, soulful, spirit-heart-mind-body voice talking to you. You're growing a new earworm — but it doesn't squawk, it sings.

To continue the tapas metaphor, this is where you really start tasting your life. You are choosing small bites, tasting a wide variety of life flavors. You are savoring the things you like, spitting out what you don't like.

Oh! Have you ever gone wine-tasting at a nice winery? The first time you go, you probably see some guy standing up at the wine bar, swirling the wine in the glass, holding it up to the light, tilting the glass, sticking his nose in the glass, taking a sip and swishing it around in his mouth, making disgusting mouth noises. And then, he spits the wine out! You probably thought, "OMG! What a pretentious horse's ass. Who is he trying to impress?" It's okay, I don't judge you. It was your first time. He's not trying to impress anyone. He's a wine enthusiast, lost in his own world, and he's absolutely enjoying the experience fully. When he swirls the glass, he's adding air to release the bouquet. When he holds it up to the light, he's using his eyes to enjoy the color and the density, and watching the legs of wine run down the sides of the glass. He's using his nose to smell the wine, because the sense of smell is so closely integrated with the sense of taste. He takes a sip and moves it all around his mouth to see what the wine feels like in his mouth and to find all the different layers of tastes — because we taste different things on different places on our tongues. Then he spits it out, because he doesn't want the alcohol in the wine to impair his judgment just yet — and also because he wants to see what his mouth tastes and feels like afterwards (the finish). I hope you can see how he's not pretentious, just fully and totally enjoying the moment. If you have done this, because you are a wine geek, I bet as you read this paragraph you were reliving the experience of tasting a really wonderful Napa cab or a Sonoma pinot or chard or something. I was! (Okay, I know, sometimes he really is a horse's ass, trying to impress someone, acting all wine-connoisseury and shit.)

Well, that was a nice little trip to the wine country, but back to *your* journey. I want you to take each item on your list as seriously as that hipster wine geek guy did, and do the equivalent of the swirl, stare, sniff, sip, spit thing — whatever that is for you.

Oh yeah… trust yourself. Trust that your mind and your intuition will keep you safe. Trust your judgment. Trust that your body and your heart will tell you what you like and what is good for you. Trust your instincts to tell you what to try. Remember, you are tasting! One thing might lead to another. Once you get on a path, trust your intuition on where to go next. As my friend Velva says, "Trust your instinct. It's your spirit giving you directions."

Along the way, you'll find people to whom you are immensely attracted. You'll find people who believe what you really believe, think what you think. Or maybe they challenge your thinking and you love that. Or maybe they make you feel safe — and you crave safety and acceptance. Maybe they have what you want. Maybe they express themselves the way you want to express yourself. They might even be your age or older — and they're doing things you want to do. That's awesome. They just might be your next best friend, your people, your earth family, your tribe. Take note. Think of more ways to connect with them and put those ideas on your options list.

Above all else, *think for yourself*. You don't need a leader on this step of the journey. You're not following anyone. Don't follow "the experts" — they don't know you like you now know you (I'm glad that's not a song!). Believe what *you* believe, feel what *you* feel, say what *you* think. If you hear someone say "should," make like brave Sir Robin and run away. Seriously, while you are doing research, especially in the thoughts and beliefs areas, keep in mind that you are probably going to come across some highly influential speakers. Remember that *they* believe in what they are saying. You might find it interesting, you might pick up your one thing from them. For now, keep a bit of a distance. Even if you really, really like something or someone, don't go whole hog down that rabbit hole and invest in the week-long, life-changing training series. Put it on your list of things that you like, call it a favorable option and know that you might explore it later. You are still in research mode, focusing on adding to and narrowing down your list of options; gathering the data on what you like and don't like. Of course you are going to commit and buy and join — but that comes later. You'll make decisions in the next step.

What kind of stuff are you trying out? Anything that is on your list from the last step. Anything that you think of that you want to try. This isn't about finding the new, magical career that will change your life. Well, maybe it is, but only if that's what you really want. You are so much more than how you get paid to spend your time. This is about you as a whole person — mind, body, heart, soul, spirit — remember? What makes you feel alive? What do you want to add to your life? It can be about work, sure, but it can also be about hobbies, art, relationships, music, spiritual practices, magic, colors, travels, landscapes, foods, aromas, etc. It can include new discoveries or rediscoveries. You can be reunited with yourself, old friends or old practices that you haven't made time for in a long time. The point is to try things that you think might help you be a better, happier, more complete and aligned version of yourself.

Man, I'm hungry. Well, not really hungry, but I want to get some good tastes in my mouth. I need to get to a tapas bar! I know, I'll go to ZuZus and order the salted cod, and the olives, and the artichoke dip, and the paella and....

How long is this step? Well, I think I lied a little bit when I said that the first step, J — Just Who Are You, was the longest. I really did intend for it to be the longest chapter, but, well, stuff happens. In my 12-week transformation program, we do spend six weeks on getting to know you. But we spend all 12 weeks picking things from the Tapas Menu and exploring and researching and trying things out. I just don't tell you why we're doing it. So if you end up working with me and going through the program, you'll have a head start. It's okay. It's not like I have to keep it a surprise or anything.

So how long is this step? I really hope it lasts for the rest of your natural life. I hope you are tasting life, following your curiosity and getting inspiration forever. From here on, the rest of the steps are kind of an iterative process, an endless loop of living life to the fullest. Whoops. I let that cat out of the bag. Shoot. Okay, I'll fess up. You are already in the process of fulfilling your potential. In fact, I hope that by now you are so distracted that you've completely forgotten about your original question or problem because you feel so alive and curious. Did I maybe trick you? Just a little? Yes. Please don't be mad. I didn't manipulate you. I came and found you where you were. If I had said, "Hey come out and play! There's a whole world of stuff to try, and you just need to start trying it and you'll feel better," you probably would have said something like, "This isn't the book for me." Remember, you still had the squawking earworm of discontent, telling you some bullshit about how it's too late, you haven't come close to reaching your potential, your life is over, you're a failure and the world is in the hands of those kids. I hope that's just a vague memory by now. Of course, if you are reading the book straight through, I want you to picture how you'll feel when you actually do the J-O-U-R steps.

"Maggie, really, will you tell me how long this step takes!!??!!" Yes, yes, fine. As you go along this JOURNEY process, spend as much time as you are comfortable spending testing things out. When you feel like you are good enough at testing stuff out, and you can really hear *your* voice telling you what you do and don't like, and you can easily tune out the impersonator voices that tell you what you *should* do, then ta da! You are ready to move on. You don't have to be perfect, right? Just kinda ready. Your gut will tell you when you feel like it is time to make some choices. And I want you to make choices and decisions, because they are just as important as research. In fact... making choices is one of your superpowers!

EXERCISES:

Build your own Tapas Menu. Create your own sheet or use one of mine from my website. You can make it really fun and pretty, or do it as a checklist. It doesn't matter. It's what *you* want to make it. The requirements are that the items are actions, that they are small and you can do them in a few minutes a day or over a week. For example, if one of your items to research is to explore creative writing to see if you might like it as a career, you wouldn't put "write a book" on your menu. You'd put several small things on your menu: "Watch YouTube shorts on creative writing," "Google to find jump lines," "write for 15 minutes at different times of the day," "read some short stories by different authors to check out genres," "write the same short story from different points of view." Get the picture? Think of lots of little things around the topic that can give you some tasty little bites. Hint: If you try a couple of bites about a topic and find that you don't really like that topic much after all, you don't have to do everything else you wrote on your list about it. Trust your judgment. But if you think of more things to try, about different topics, add them to your menu. Below are some ideas in each category to get your juices flowing.

Mind:

- Explore Colette Baron-Reid on her website: www.colettebaronreid.com
  - on YouTube: www.youtube.com/user/Colette BaronReid
  - on Facebook: www.facebook.com/cbr.psychic

- Intellectually explore the concept and science behind intuition

- Research the gut/brain connection

- Explore time theory — watch *Interstellar*, Google Stephen Hawking's stuff on time, read Madeleine l'Engle's novel *A Wrinkle in Time*

- Research a belief you have that you suspect just might not be true

Body:

- Try a mindful activity as exercise at least two times this week (yoga, Pilates, stretching, walking, etc.)

- Try a new food every day and write about it

- Try different practices that facilitate sleep

- Set an intention to dream and remember the dream

Heart:

- Practice using distancing techniques to separate from emotionally charged situations

- Look into an "alternative" healing modality; schedule a visit to a practitioner of one that interests you and journal about the experience

Spirit:

- Do breath work (see my site for some examples)

- Try meditation

- Try guided meditation

- Check out chakra tuning (if you don't have a tool for doing this, search for it on Google or YouTube)

Soul:

- Start doing Morning Pages from *The Artist's Way*, by Julia Cameron; she has a short video of instructions on her website

- Start collecting inspiration — from anywhere and everywhere: images for a collage, quotes you like, YouTube videos that inspire you, songs that make you happy; cut, tear, photocopy, Pin, copy... don't categorize, just collect

- Listen to music: Make a list of songs that make you feel good and describe how they make you feel; notice different textures and ways to feel good

- Make a temporary tattoo of a word, symbol or phrase that reminds you of good things, of being happy, of taking care of yourself, feeling gratitude, etc.

- Write about everything you do. In your journal, make sure you write down what you think, how you feel, what comes up for you at the time you try something and afterward, what you dream about. Spend some time in free flow mode, too.

Remember to write down on your blank cards any truth or insight you discover.

Summing it all up:

Things to remember:

- Try things out before you commit.

- It's okay to spit.

- Really savor the process.

- Follow your intuition.

- Think for yourself.

Ready to try a new super power? Go get your cape!

📖✍ FIELD NOTES ✍📖

What are some ideas you have for your own personal tapas menu? MIND: ideas, theories, truths you want to explore

---

☐ ✐ FIELD NOTES ✐ ☐

BODY: foods, tastes, movement, rest, dreams, self-care, healing, cleansing, etc.

FIELD NOTES

HEART: emotions, healing and relationships you want to explore

---

SPIRIT: beliefs, values, rituals, practices, energy work, meditations, prayer, faith communities, etc.

SOUL: How do you want to explore or cultivate creative talents, inspiration or expression?

Chapter 7.

N - Now Make Some Choices

"Decision is the force that shapes destiny."

~ Tony Robbins

Choice and decision aren't exactly the same things. You can make an intellectual decision, and have no conviction behind it. Have you ever done that? It can seem a lot like settling — and how far from powerful does *that* feel? But making a choice is different. Choosing combines the deliberation of a decision with the intention to carry through, to make something happen. Choice is where our power begins.

Key Concepts

Making real choices takes practice. Sometimes we're out of practice or stuck or lost or just kinda forgot all about our power because life has happened (and we let it happen). That's why you first started hearing the earworm of discontent.

Words matter. Words are the building blocks of thoughts. Words are the bricks that we use to create. "Words are things," says Maya Angelou. Choose your building materials carefully. Look at the words you use frequently and make sure they are the things you want to hear in your voice and the stuff you want to use to build your truth.

Thoughts have power and energy. If you ask Nikola Tesla, everything is energy and the secrets of the universe are found in energy, frequency and vibration. Thoughts *are* energy they carry a positive or a negative charge. That's one aspect of the power of thought.

Another aspect is that *thoughts, when repeated, become beliefs*. Beliefs drive behavior, action and emotion. Beliefs don't have to be true ("The world is flat."). By the time something has become a belief, we may not even be aware of it anymore (beliefs about our self-worth are often like this), yet our beliefs inform our entire view of the world. This can be positive or negative, right?

Beliefs drive our decisions. And as Tony Robbins says, "Decisions drive our destiny." I'm going to add that *beliefs drive our choices*.

Choice and power are intimately related. I'm not talking about world-domination-type power or political power or power over other people. I'm talking about personal power — filling up your skin with confidence, competence, strength, purpose, authenticity and commitment.

Personal power feels good. It feels strong, in control, energized, and... well, powerful! Feeling powerless is the worst. It sucks. It feels like we're trapped, have no say, options or choice in life, and it totally saps our energy. See, that's why I said what I did in that last chapter about where the earworm came from! Ironically, it is when we are powerless that we have to muster everything we have in order to be strong enough to get through. It's just so damned hard — no wonder we want to give up and wait for the fairy godmother to come fix everything.

This step is all about making choices. Yay!!! Finally, you get to use your first superpower! And you get to choose some new super powers, too.

Making a choice doesn't shut other doors. Ironically, it opens up a whole host of new possibilities. When I was majorly trapped, listening to the damned earworm every night, one of the lies I told myself was that I wasn't making choices because I was keeping my options open. Such complete bullshit.

I discovered that was bullshit purely by accident. I was in the pit of despair. I hated my job. That was when I really was the Mistress of Broken Shit. My job was literally fixing broken processes and writing massive weekly PowerPoint decks to convince the Überbosses that we were making progress, or we needed more money or that we knew what we were doing and didn't need to bring in a bunch of "help" from the home office. I had been complaining to my boss for a while, asking for something new to do, something more challenging and a lot more fun. He kept looking at me blankly and handing me more messed up things to fix. He didn't do that because he didn't care about me or my career; he did it because he had no idea what to do with me, what would make me happy, and he wasn't my fairy godmother. Oh yeah, and he had a bunch of broken shit that needed fixing.

I spent lots of time trying to figure out how to get him to give me a promotion out of there, but I couldn't come up with any ideas. I thought about going on the market and getting a new job. But I just could make any choices about what to do.

One day, I was especially frustrated. It was a Thursday and my boss was out of the office, down in Napa at a three-day senior management meeting of some sort. I decided "F**k it, I'm getting a tattoo" and I spent the morning looking at images of Celtic ring designs for a tattoo. I chose one that I really, really loved, made an appointment and left work an hour early to go get a tattoo. You need to know that I didn't have any tattoos and this was a big deal to me. So this was a *huge* choice for me.

I was driving to go get my tattoo and my boss called me. He was still in his big pow-wow, but he had stepped outside to call me. "Hey, can you go to Melbourne this weekend? There's this thing that came up." (We were going through a big demerger from our former parent company.) "It's about the IT transition and we need

someone to help with the strategy and staffing and stuff."
(He's not at all technical — it gives him a headache). "I
was talking to Rita..." (VP of IT at the time) "... and you
could really help her."

Boom. My world changed. One week later I was in Melbourne, on the transition team, and we were planning the IT strategy for the future of our company. One of my favorite pictures in the world was taken on a Saturday in the office of the former CEO. It's a picture of my feet up on his desk. I'm wearing purple Converse All Stars and purple jeans, and they are framed by this beautiful wood desk. That picture is way better than a tattoo. It commemorates the launch of a whole new career growth spurt that opened so many doors for me.

No, I never did get the tattoo. I didn't need to. But I know for a fact that when I finally made a choice, a big choice with some conviction and skin in the game (tattoo joke, sorry) I stepped into my power. That power went out into the universe and opened up doors for me, doors that I didn't even know were possibilities. So that's the story of how I learned that making one choice does not limit your options.

Now, I can't promise or predict what doors will open for you, or what kind of choices you need to make. After all, it's your life and your story; they're your doors and your choices. What I can promise you is that you will begin to feel your power seep back into your body with every choice you make. So get crackin', mate!

You have your list of things that you liked and didn't like from the R — Research step. Take that list and make some choices about what you are going to let into your life, what you will actively pursue and what you might stop.

And now, as promised, here is a guide to choosing your own custom super powers.

Mind: Choose your words and your thoughts. If a thought is negatively charged or doesn't serve you, stop thinking it. If you start to go there, say, "Cancel, cancel," and hit the mental delete button, or just follow it up with something like, "That's not true," and intentionally move on to a more positively charged thought. From there, you can choose how you are going to spend your brain time — what you're going to read, hear, watch and think about. *What you think is one of your super powers.*

Body: Choose your lifestyle. What health goals do you want to have? What kind of food and drink do you take in? What might you want to give up, and what do you want to add? What kind of movement do you want to do — what kind of exercise? What do you want to do about stress, sleep, toxins? Maybe you have an addiction you want to address? *Choosing to live to support your personal version of healthy is a superpower.*

Heart: Choose your tribe. Choose which relationships get more time in your life and which get less. Maybe choose to change the types of relationships you have. Maybe you want to choose groups to join. You can also choose how you want to feel. It's a longer topic that's worth exploring later on your own, for sure, but you can always start with choosing to do things around gratitude. Gratitude is the alchemist for emotions. *Choosing how you feel, especially how you love, is a superpower.*

Spirit: Choose your beliefs and practices. You might not think you have any, and so you might choose to add some. Or you might choose to make a big change. You might choose to add some daily rituals, like meditation, journaling, creating gratitude lists, praying or whatever speaks to you. *Choosing what you believe is a superpower.*

Soul: Choose your art, your creative expression and your voice. Choose your story carefully, being very intentional about what you say and think about yourself from this point forward. You can choose to let go of things that are no longer true. *Choose your story, your gifts and your talents. They are super powers.*

EXERCISES:

Observe how you choose stuff. Take something simple that you have to do often, such as eating dinner or lunch, and practice different ways of choosing what to have. Choose by listening to your gut, by what looks pretty, by research or by using your body as a pendulum — whatever ways you can come up with. Give up your power by letting someone else choose for you. How does that feel?

Let your soul play with creativity. Write a story about yourself as a super hero. What are your superpowers? What enemies or adversity do you face? Who do you protect? How do you save the world? Do you wear a costume? Do you have a secret identity? Play with this and have fun! Illustrate your discoveries with a picture of yourself as a super hero.

Remember to write down on your blank cards any truth or insight you discover.

Here's a story about my mom. It's a hard story, but it's beautiful. A few years ago, our long-time family friend, Mikey, needed a kidney transplant. My mom was a very young and vibrant 72, in great health, and wanted to donate one of her kidneys. She was told that she was too old, and they wouldn't take her kidney. That really made her mad, and my mom could hold a grudge.

My mom was a *huge* San Francisco Giants fan. In 2012, the Giants had a spectacular year and were in the playoffs. I bought tickets for us to go to a playoff game. They were just about the best seats you could buy. I really wanted to splurge for something wonderful for my mom. She was so excited. She kept calling it a "once in a lifetime" event, even though we had been to playoffs and even to World Series games before.

The Giants were winning, and in the top of the ninth

inning, my mom said she wanted to start walking towards the ferry because she was getting a headache. That wasn't like her, but we got up and left and started walking towards the ferry, still paying a little attention to the game. When we got on the ferry and sat down, my mom said she was scared, that this was the worst headache she'd ever had. I got help, the paramedics came, carried my mom off the ferry, and got her into an ambulance. She was unconscious and unresponsive by then. The ambulance driver hurried as best as he could through the huge crowd of fans and took her to San Francisco General Hospital.

About 20 minutes after she was admitted, the ER neurosurgeon told me that my mom had had a catastrophic aneurism. I knew what that meant. I told her that my mother really wanted to be an organ donor. We were able to work that out. My mom was able to donate both of her kidneys, her liver and her heart. She passed her life on to three more families.

The doctor told me I had a decision to make. But I really didn't, because my mom had made the choice already. She chose how, where and when she died. She chose to die in a manner and in a place that made it possible for her to be an organ donor. And she chose to die after the ninth inning of a Giants' playoff game, so she still saw the whole game. She got her "once in a lifetime" event.

Yes, it was hard and traumatic for me. Sometimes I thought she was pretty selfish for putting me through the whole thing. Of course, that was the grief talking. But I never doubted that my mom — in her deepest soul — had made a powerful, generous choice. No one in our family ever second-guessed her "decision," because she had told us all what she wanted. Her choice was her superpower, and she really was a heroine.

Summing it all up:

What I want you to remember:

- Words, thoughts and beliefs really matter.

- You can trust yourself to make good choices.

- Choice is phenomenally empowering.

- Making one choice does not shut all other doors.

- Personal power feels really, really good.

Now let's move on to making a plan to set some of your big choices in motion.

How do you make choices? What are some big choices you've made in the past? What choices might be in the near future? How are you going to make them?

Choose your superpowers

Trigger words: empowered, strong, clear, tribe, healthy, clean, organic, toxins, stress, play, sport, laugh, conviction, people, family, friends, love, frustration, productive, accomplishment, music, paint, story, craft, memories, action, nature, grounding, energy, nurture, choice, decision, action, pause, patience, perspective, attitude, words

MIND: Do you use words that you'd like to stop using? What are they and why? What are some powerful, positively charged words you'd like to add to your thoughts and vocabulary?

BODY: What is your personal version of a healthy you? What healthy goals do you have? What's your highest priority? What do you want to add in or crowd out? What's your lifestyle?

HEART: What are you feeling here? What feelings do you want more or less of in your life? Which relationships do you want to give more time, and which ones less? If you get stuck, try some emotional alchemy: make a gratitude list, taking time to FEEL gratitude for everything on the list. Now, what you want more of??

✍ FIELD NOTES ✍

SPIRIT: What do you believe, what do you value? Do you have any rituals? Daily practices? Do you want to add any? What beliefs — especially about yourself — need to be updated?

SOUL: What are your special gifts and talents? How do you want to express your creativity? What does your soul's voice sound like? How do you want to tell your story? What do you want to change in your story?

Chapter 8.

E — Establish A Plan

"I don't have to figure out everything to figure out anything."

~ Lauren Russo (Structured Freedom)

The original title for this step was going to be "E — Eek, You Need a Plan!" but I knew that would scare you off, so I used a more grown-up title. But a grown-up title won't take away the "eek" elements in planning. I hope this chapter helps! If you're already an expert planner, feel free to point and laugh along the way!

So why do you need a plan? Oh, don't even go there. You know why you need a plan. Because you want to get something done, and you want to be successful and you don't want to be surprised. And you want to be able to sleep at night because you know what you have to do next.

Do you need a plan for everything? Of course not. When do you need a plan? It depends. (That's my favorite answer!) Let's say you want to learn Spanish. Why you want to learn it can help decide whether you need a plan or not, by putting it in context.

Say you want to learn Spanish because you think know-ing another language would be fun, or because you live in California and it would be really useful to be bilingual. Do you need a plan? Not really — "learn Spanish" is pretty much an action item all on its own.

Say you want to learn some conversational Spanish because you'd like to take a trip to Spain next summer. Plan? Probably not. It's an action item on a to-do list, along with "renew passport" and "make travel reserva-tions" and "research museums," and the like.

Or, say you want to learn Spanish because you want to move to Spain next September. Do you need a plan? I would say so. But the plan would be for the move, and learning Spanish would be part of the plan.

You've already chosen the *what* — you did that in the last step. There were probably one or two big changes you decided you want to make, a goal or two that you want to pursue — and they are big enough that you think a plan would be helpful.

This step is the *how* — how are you going to achieve your goal? You figure that out as you make the plan. There might be a few decisions and choices you have to make along the way that come up as you dive into the details of the plan. But, guess what? You know how to do that now, because choosing is one of your super powers!

I told you back in Chapter 2 that change management is a big factor in whether or not corporate projects are successful. I can tell you that the second most important factor is planning. A good plan really sets you up to succeed because it helps you set and manage realistic expectations; it lines up the time, money and other resources you need; and it lays out a clear timeline. A plan serves as a baseline that helps you see the progress you're making, and it's super helpful when you need to adjust — because things always change! The lack of a good plan — or worse, having a bad plan — has turned fantastic projects into disasters. A bad plan is usually just not achievable, because it's built on unrealistic goals, timelines, assumptions or resource requirements. In a corporate context, a bad plan usually is created because an executive simply says, "Make it work," and insists on some utterly ridiculous constraints and doesn't give the support necessary to actually *make it work*. Simply put, a good plan is achievable, a bad plan isn't.

I've suggested that a personal change management strategy could be pretty helpful. You can see where this is going, right? Learning from the kinds of mistakes that are made in a business context and having some planning skills can be pretty nifty, too.

There are all kinds of resources to teach you how to plan in gory detail. I think you only need them if one of your choices is to become a planner, a project manager or to do some other vocation that requires delivering detailed plans. Not you? So, on a personal level, you aren't worried about getting fired for screwing up a big, expensive project. But you do want to succeed, right? In that case, the kinds of things you want to avoid are:

- Not planning at all; just jumping into action

- Planning in too much detail; never getting into action

- Making a plan so rigid that you can't adjust

- Making a plan so unrealistic that you fail before you start

- Not planning for what you need, and running out of time or money

- Not letting other people know the plan

What you need for this step is just enough information to figure out how to put some structure together to help you get your choices converted into actions without a bunch of chaos, drama and panic. You want the Goldilocks planning system, the one that's just right!

I want to give you enough tools here to help you find that happy balance.

Key Concepts

A plan is not a to-do list. A plan is a list of actions that you need to do in a set amount of time, in the order that you need to do them in, and a list of the stuff you need in order to be able to do the actions so that you can achieve the goal.

Goals are the things you want to achieve — the end points. They are the desired results of your ambition.

A timeline represents the amount of time you think it will take to achieve the goal, or the amount of time you have, if there's a deadline.

Milestones are points where you complete a significant achievement or event as you move from one stage to the next. Don't go too granular on the milestones. There are no hard and fast rules on milestones. Choosing them really depends upon the overall context and timeline. For example, if your goal is finishing a semester in school, your milestones would probably be major events like the due dates for papers, projects, midterms and finals. If your goal is getting a diploma, semesters or years and required courses would probably be your milestones.

A plan is made up of **steps** that are action items. A plan is a list of things you have to do, in the order that you have to do them. Steps are not goals; steps are actions. A step is a bite-sized chunk of activity. You only need to go down to the level of detail that makes sense to you. Steps aren't always sequential; you can have several things going on at once (another reason for having a plan, right?).

Assumptions are exactly what they sound like — the things that you have to assume, for now — because you won't have solid info until some later time. If you write down your assumptions, you can make adjustments to the plan when you find out more. It's a lot easier to write them down now than it is to try to remember them in a few months when you have to recalculate something! Assumptions are things like how long something will take, how much it will cost, and the order you're going to do things.

Deliverables are a concept that is handy. Deliverables are things that you have to give to someone else as the result of some of your steps. For example, in writing my book, the first draft of my manuscript is a deliverable. You want to keep track of them so that you don't miss them.

Resources are things that you need in order to achieve the plan. They are usually things like time set aside on your calendar, money, space, tools, equipment and people. When you're making a plan, it's a really good idea to think through and make a list of what resources it will take to get the plan done.

Now let's talk about how you actually make your plan. As I mentioned before, try not to make it harder than it needs to be. If you really do need something to help you manage a more intricate project or set of projects, I suggest that when you look for resources, keep your eyes out for a good hack. You can check out lifehacker.com for some good software recommendations. Or, even better, I *highly* recommend that you check out Lauren Russo and her Structured Freedom approach www.laurendrusso.com/structured-freedom.

There's a chance that you are a true visionary, the kind of person who comes up with fabulous ideas but has no idea (or interest) in how to get things done. Details make your head hurt. You think it's quite possible that birds did sew Cinderella's ball gown. You know what? You need help... help to plan, that is. Finding a service provider — a personal planning service or a specialized planner (think wedding planner model) — could really help set you up for success. But, for now, let's assume you have at least some head for details, and I'll give you the lay of the land.

How do you make a plan? You answer questions and write down the answers in the order the key concepts above are listed. Use whatever format you'd like — list, chart, spreadsheet, etc.

1. What's the goal? What is it, specifically, that you are trying to achieve? That's your endpoint.

2. What's the timeline? How much time do you have to get it done? If you don't have a deadline, when would you like to hit the goal?

3. What are the major milestones you will want to achieve along the way? Where do they fit on the timeline? Tease out the milestones. A good rule of thumb is that it takes five to ten steps to hit a milestone.

4. What are the steps it will take to accomplish each milestone? Think through the order — what needs to happen first? Guesstimate how long each step might take. It's okay to adjust the timeline as you learn more.

5. What are the deliverables? When are they due? List them as steps, but you probably want to highlight them or keep them on a separate list, too.

6. What else are you going to need to get this done? Money, space, tools, equipment, help from other people?

7. Keep track of the assumptions you used to figure out how long the steps were going to take, how much things will cost, etc.

8. Do a sanity check to make sure the steps can be done in the time allotted. If it doesn't seem like it will work, something's gotta give, so move things around until the plan works.

9. Review the plan. Get feedback from someone helpful. Adjust the plan until it makes sense.

10. Once the plan looks good, stop planning and start doing!

That's the theory, and it does work.

Here are my two favorite hacks for planning:

1. Use yellow stickies. Actually, they can be any color. I really like to use color-coding to distinguish between steps, milestones and random info. I pretty much use stickies for any thing that needs a bit of structure. I jot down the pieces of the plan I already know first, add things as I think of them, and rearrange them until a structure emerges. This works really well for planning.

You can move things around easily, and you don't get too attached to your initial drafts!

2. Work backwards! Start with your final goal and ask what needs to happen right before that? Keep working backward, listing all the steps, asking, "What is the step right before this?" Once you have all the steps, you can pretty easily identify the milestones and durations. I think this works well for me because I like to de-construct things. Test out how reasonable your plan is by reconstructing it. Talk it through to yourself from front to back this time - out loud, as if you are presenting it to someone else. Doing it out loud is important, because you really do notice more things that might need to be adjusted when you have to put the whole thing into words. And if you use funny accents, you can really keep yourself entertained. Or you can actually present it to someone else and get their feedback — that's even better.

When I combine both hacks, I find that I get through the whole planning process a lot quicker and my final plan is way more robust.

You can make it that simple or you can make it a whole lot more complicated, but why would you? By now you should know that if it's going to work, you have to do what works for you!

You need a plan, but you don't have to figure out all the details at once at the beginning. You can come up with a high-level plan, and work out the next level of details one milestone at a time. In fact, if you find that you are making a lot of assumptions and you think that your plan might bite you in the ass later if you get too detailed this soon, it's a really practical approach to build detail as you go. Because life happens and plans can change. Plans do change! It's actually more useful to be good at planning than it is to have a perfect plan. When things come up — and they do - you don't want to go crazy and have things fall apart just because you have to change your plans. You want to be able to be fluid and resilient enough to make the adjustments and keep on going forward.

Remember to write down on your blank cards any truth or insight you discover.

Summing it all up:

• Good planning can make you successful.

• A good plan is realistic.

• What's the best way to get good at planning? Practice planning.

• Be prepared for plans to change!

• Why do we plan? So that we can do what we want to do without a whole lot of drama, chaos and fear.

What's the next step? Taking inspired actions!

FIELD NOTES

So what are you going to do? What are your goals, milestones and timelines? Do you need a plan?

📖✎ FIELD NOTES ✎📖

What are your inspired action steps? What are your very next steps? Or, what's your first step?

📖✎ FIELD NOTES ✎📖

Whose help do you want or need?
Do you need any other resources?

FIELD NOTES

Do you have any quick hits or to-do items?

- [ ]
- [ ]
- [ ]
- [ ]
- [ ]
- [ ]
- [ ]
- [ ]
- [ ]
- [ ]
- [ ]
- [ ]
- [ ]
- [ ]
- [ ]
- [ ]
- [ ]
- [ ]

Chapter 9.

Y — You, in Inspired Action

"You want a miracle? Be the miracle."

~ God (as played by Morgan Freeman in *Bruce Almighty*)

In the last chapter, we talked about planning and you identified steps that you are going to take. I told you that those were actions — and that's true. But I want to introduce one more set of concepts that will put a little magic into the things you do and the steps you take. Maybe there's no such thing as a fairy godmother (and I'm only saying maybe), but there is such a thing as magic!

Key Concepts

Synchronicity and flow. When we are working from our own place of power, we know who we are, what we believe and what we want. We recognize and take care of all aspects of our being — mind, body, heart, spirit and soul. We are living up to our true potential because we are living as spiritual beings in a physical body. When that happens we experience synchronicity and flow all over the place. Life is just easier than it was. You don't feel like it's a struggle to feel good and be happy. It seems like things just line up, and what you are looking for seems to appear magically before you. This is the part where my friend Elizabeth shakes her booty, celebrating a-bun-dance.

Inspired Action. When we want something to happen, we take action — but how do we know what is the right action? When we are in our power and flow, we experience inspired action. It's like getting little flashlights on our feet that light up the next steps on our path. We can see clearly and we just know what feels right. The entire journey may not be lit up, but we know what to do now.

Trust in miracles. Miracles *do* happen. I've had so many I can't count them. When I look in the rear view mirror, it's easy to trace backward and see the chain of cause and effect that explains how they happened. Sometimes (but not always) it's even possible to see the inspired action that was the catalyst for making all the miracles happen. Don't think for a moment that just because you can look in the rear view mirror and understand how it happened that it wasn't a miracle! Looking forward, hoping for a miracle, it's not really possible to see what the catalyst will be or how the chain of cause and effect might ripple out. The miracle will still happen, so sit back and expect miracles. You'll get the explanation later. Looking forward, it's just, well, it's just miraculous.

Calling, Purpose, Career, or Vocation. "What am I here to do?" we ask, as if there were only one answer. There are definitions for and distinctions between the words *calling, purpose, career* and *vocation*. Ultimately, it doesn't matter which word means what. The relevant questions about them are something like: "Why am I here?" "What am I here to give to the world, to get from this life, to do with my time and to earn my keep?" "What can I, should I, must I, may I do for a full life?" and "What do I want to do?" By now, you've chosen answers to some of these questions and you have the ability and the desire and the powers to go find more answers!

How big is your world? Most of us want to make a difference. Maybe we've been told that we were given great gifts and talents and we have an obligation to do something really big with them. Maybe we want to "save the world," but when we find out how hard that is or how much we have to sacrifice to do it, we suddenly feel very small and question our worth. We might even we feel *guilty* for not living up to our intellectual potential - or our athletic or artistic or other specific gifts. The reality is that you are one person with one life. One of the most liberating choices we can make is to decide how big our world is. We can set the boundaries on our world, and unleash the full force of all of our gifts and talents on that world. And we can rest assured, knowing that there are other worlds in our universe — and other talented people going about the business of saving them.

If you take all of these key concepts and roll them into one thing, you get a big ball of sparkly light that is *you*, living in inspired action and fulfilling your potential (as if that even matters anymore), being a better and better version of yourself every day. And that matters very, very much. Do you get now that your potential never was and never will be a list of your achievements? Your potential is about who you are, how you live and how your soul expresses your creative life force!

EXERCISE:

Take all of the index cards — you know, the ones where you wrote something that was an insight, an "aha," a "duh," or something that was especially true for you? The ones I reminded you about in each chapter? Okay, go through them one at a time. Throw out any that are no longer true. What's left is your own special oracle card deck. You can randomly pick a card when you feel like you need some special advice from your intuition. You can add any affirmations or insights as you go along in life and the deck will grow.

Okay, let's check in one last time. If you've gotten this far, you've read the book. Did you do the exercises? Do you have a plan? If the answer is yes, please, please go put on your favorite music and celebrate with a-bun-dance! Look at where you are now! And you're going to do and feel and be so much more yourself every day.

If the answer is no, here's what's going to happen: not

much. You'll be enthusiastic and hopeful for a little while and then it'll fade away. If that's okay with you, then fine. If you made a conscious choice that this J-O-U-R-N-E-Y isn't for you, that's great, because that is you exercising your power of choice. But know that you really haven't done anything to get yourself out of this quagmire of stuck-ness that you are in, and you won't until you make a choice to take some kind of action. So keep looking until you find what you need, please!

If you didn't make a choice — if you were just lazy or scared or distracted or whatever — then look at it this way: You've already invested a bunch of time in this book, and the problem that brought you to it hasn't magically gone away, has it?

So, here are your options:

- Do nothing and this can be like all the other times you've scanned something like a book without taking action. The earworm of discontent may go dormant, but it'll be back.

- Go back and do the steps to give yourself a fair shot at shutting up the damned earworm.

- Call me. Let's talk to see if you think we could do this together. Sometimes it is hard to stay out of your own bullshit when doing this kind of work. Working with a coach can really help you move through things faster and stay accountable to your goals. Working with a coach keeps you doing the exercises in integrity, as they are meant to be done, with a witness and experienced guidance around whatever comes up in the process. Or if you want help but don't think individual coaching is your next step, do the Tapas for Your Soul group program. It's very similar to the one-on-one program, except it has group coaching calls, online materials and a Facebook group. You can find out more about all of those options at www.TalktoMaggie.com.

How big do you want your world to be?
Remember, this is a decision that you get to make!

📖✎ FIELD NOTES ✎📖

Check In. Did you do the exercises? If yes, how do you feel about what you've done? Is it enough or will you continue to do more?

If no, did you make a choice? What have you decided to do?

How will you hold yourself accountable? What are you going to do to be VERY successful this time?

Who will be excited and support you on your journey? Who would be fun to take along?

How do you feel right now? If you like how you feel, how are you going to hang on to this feeling? If you don't like how you feel, what are you going to do to change it?

Epilogue
Chapter 10

— The Love Letter

As I've been writing this book, I have really been thinking about you. I've come to love you — a lot! I want to share one more thing with you. Before I started this book, I wrote you a letter. I want to share it with you so you know what was in my heart as I wrote this book.

Dear lovely, wonderful, radiant reader:

I want so much for you! I want this book to touch you and to give you something that you really, really want. Only you know what you really want. Maybe you are in touch with it right now. Maybe you aren't. Maybe you want to know what you want. Maybe you feel a bit anesthetized and want to want something again. Maybe you think you're totally dead inside. Maybe you think you missed all of the opportunities and there really isn't much left for you besides the path you've already chosen. Or maybe you have a spark of an idea, but you feel guilty for being self-indulgent and wanting something new, different, more. Maybe, maybe, maybe....

What I want for you, first of all, is a spark. I want that spark to be a spark of desire. Desire is good. Desire is what dreams are made of, right? I want you to want something passionately. And, you know what? I don't care if you want it for two seconds or two days or two years. In fact, I prefer that you only want it for a short time, because I want you to follow the path of that want and try something out. And then to have a new idea of something you want to try.

Next, I want you to be free from anxiety, but free to be afraid. Fear is a wonderful thing when we have the right attitude. Fear tells us what really matters to us. Sometimes we have to dig through a few layers to find out what the real message is, but it's there.

I want you to know that you are a complex being, with many facets: mind, body, heart, spirit and soul. I want you to know how to care for and feed all of these facets of yourself.

I want you to know that your life is like a patchwork quilt. Sometimes you can't see the pattern until you get enough pieces sewn together and you get a little distance and perspective. Your life's purpose? It's a journey, and your journey is unique. You know that cliché "It's about the journey, not the destination?" That's sooooo f'ing true.

By the end of this book, or my program if you decide to try it out, I want you to feel like you are finally on your journey. I don't want you to feel that you are stalled or stuck or settling. I want you, at every crossroads, to see opportunities. I want you to know yourself well enough to know what you like, how you make choices and how to listen to your intuition. Really, the bottom line is that I want you to be able to look in the mirror and trust the person you see. I want you to trust her to make the very best decisions for you and your life. Of course, I want you to like her a lot, too. Even if it's a secret for a while!

I want your mind to be active and interested and engaged and challenged.

I want your body to feel energetic and graceful and healthy.

I want your heart to feel love and joy and gratitude.

I want your spirit to feel a connection with your source, higher power, God — whatever is the right name for you for that spiritual connection.

I want your soul to feel like an artist with many wonderful ways to express your creative life force.

I want you to believe in magic and miracles and hopes and dreams. I want you to go to bed at night and be able to say, "Thank you," for everything you did and didn't do today. I want you to sleep the sleep of the innocent, and to dream and to remember your dreams.

I want you to be able to rattle off all of your super powers, and to know that you are the heroine of your own story! I want you to find your voice and tell your story, your new story, the stuff that's true... and to throw away all the stuff that is no longer true.

I wish you could see yourself through my eyes! You'd be so surprised at what I see, I think. You're so beautiful.

I want you to be able to have a huge Tapas Menu of things that you want to explore, and the energy to follow through and explore them. I want you to have a universe of infinite possibilities to taste — and you only have to eat the stuff you like!

Love,

Maggie

FIELD NOTES

Write a letter to yourself one year from now.

Dear future me —
I want so much for you! I want...

Love,
(sign it with a flourish!)

Acknowledgements

Writing a book is like raising a child — it takes a village! There are a few villagers that I absolutely must thank, or at least acknowledge. Mom, thank you for teaching me that, ultimately, everything is a choice — how you live and how you die. Katie, thank you for being my sister, critic, fan, and my rock. Danny, thank you for sharing Katie — and laughter- so generously. Jordan, thank you for choosing to be my son and sun and fun and the inspiration for so much. Katlyn, thank you for being so brave and true to yourself. Madison, thank you for having so much potential and reminding me of me. Morgan, you're a serial enthusiast, like me!

Dicky Bernando and Stephen Capen, thank you for being hilarious, and for letting me play with you.

Elizabeth LInebarger Clinton, thank you for introducing me to Aura-Soma and Eden and for seeing the real me. Victoria Silks, thank you for teaching me to stop chasing "certifications" and to get busy already. Carol Klesow, thank you for reminding me to stay grounded and to get out of my head. Gina Rossi and Bridget Engels, thank you for the angels and the faith. Dan, Marcia, Shirley, Mikey, Ctine and Mike — you are the most wonderful people. Thank you for helping me experience unconditional friendship.

Robert and Michael Mondavi, and Pete Mattei, thank you for providing a "golden age" for me to remember and hang on to when I doubt that work could be a fit place for humans, and thank you for the world of wine!

Ian J., David H., Stephen B., and Stuart M. — thank you... well, no, I acknowledge you for being such monstrous dickheads and reminding me what *not* to be, and for requiring me to be a living corporate conscience.

Katie Smith and Velva Felton, thank you for teaching me so much as your mentor and boss! Michele Baroody, thank you for reminding me why I don't want a real job. Allan Petker, David Irvine, Sanford Dole, Brian Sebastian — thank you for the music that gives my soul a voice. Kimberly Ayers, you secretly inspired me to write. Beth and Eliot — Beluga and IIN — I'm eternally grateful! Denise Green and Michael Kluczko... the Power of Intention and how to create your life... say no more. Rita Valois, thank you for letting me try totally new and big things.

Amy Pearson, synchronicity put you in my path, and I'm so grateful. You're just the *best* business coach for life coaches. You told me to stop getting ready and to get my butt in gear. I did!

Joshua Rosenthal, founder of Institute of Integrative Nutrition, thank you for teaching a whole generation of health coaches to see the whole person, and for the concept of fitting out.

Thank you Angela, John, Paul, Margaret, Caroline, Nancy and Kate for the most amazing book writing experience I could never have imagined! Kate, who knew we were cosmic siblings and that I would actually be excited about your editing suggestions?

Bimfee, you are my familiar and the best cat in the world!!!!

About the Author

Maggie Huffman is an Intuitive life coach. Her practice integrates elements for the mind, body, heart, soul and spirit. She is an author, teacher, motivational speaker and Aura-Soma practitioner. She is the founder of Tapas For Your Soul, a 12-week transformation program to get you tasting life, taking inspired action and fulfilling your true and full potential.

Maggie has her MA in theology and is completing her life coaching PhD. She spent twenty years as an executive in global wine companies. She led strategic transformation efforts — including performance and process improvement projects, major restructures, integrating acquisitions, demergers and major software implementations. What she learned from these projects — both the successes and the failures — led her directly to her coaching practice. She became an expert in change management, covertly incorporating many heart-centered elements. She discovered that many of the criteria for a successful business transformation translate directly into successful life transformations. Evolving into a life coach was a natural and fun transition.

Maggie lives in an imaginary world that looks suspiciously like Stars Hollow (of *Gilmore Girls* fame), with a workspace straight from the set of *The Good Witch*, except that it is in Sonoma, California, where there really isn't any snow. She frequently comes out to play, mostly as a serial poly-enthusiast, but some of the playful experiments that have stuck are ceramics, cycling, organic gardening, excellent choral music and random acts of magic.

Contact:
Maggie.huffman@outlook.com
www.TapasForYourSoul.com

difference press

Difference Press offers solopreneurs, including life coaches, healers, consultants, and community leaders, a comprehensive solution to get their books written, published, and promoted. A boutique-style alternative to self-publishing, Difference Press boasts a fair and easy-to-understand profit structure, low-priced author copies, and author-friendly contract terms. Its founder, Dr. Angela Lauria, has been bringing to life the literary ventures of hundreds of authors -in-transformation since 1994.

YOUR DELICIOUS BOOK

Your Delicious Book is a trailblazing program for aspiring authors who want to create a non-fiction book that becomes a platform for growing their business or communicating their message to the world in a way that creates a difference in the lives of others.

In a market where hundreds of thousands books are published every year and never heard from again, all of The Author Incubator participants have bestsellers that are actively changing lives and making a difference. The program, supported by quarterly Difference Press book-marketing summits, has a proven track record of helping aspiring authors write books that matter. Our team will hold your hand from idea to impact, showing you how to write a book, what elements must be present in your book for it to deliver the results you need, and how to meet the needs of your readers. We give you all the editing, design, and technical support you need to ensure a high-quality book published to the Kindle platform. Plus, authors in the program are connected to a powerful community of authors-in-transformation and published bestselling authors.

TACKLING THE TECHNICAL ASPECTS OF PUBLISHING

The comprehensive coaching, editing, design, publishing, and marketing services offered by Difference Press mean that your book will be edited by a pro, designed by an experienced graphic artist, and published digitally and in print by publishing industry experts. We handle all of the technical aspects of your book's creation so you can spend more of your time focusing on your business.

APPLY TO WRITE WITH US

To submit an application to our acquisitions team visit www.YourDeliciousBook.com.

Confessions of an Unlikely Runner: A Guide to Racing and Obstacle Courses for the Averagely Fit and Halfway Dedicated

by Dana L. Ayers

Matter: How to Find Meaningful Work That's Right for You and Your Family

by Caroline Greene

Reclaiming Wholeness: Letting Your Light Shine Even If You're Scared to Be Seen

by Kimberlie Chenoweth

The Well-Crafted Mom: How to Make Time for Yourself and Your Creativity within the Midst of Motherhood

by Kathleen Harper

Lifestyle Design for a Champagne Life: Find Out Why the Law of Attraction Isn't Working, Learn the Secret to Lifestyle Design, and Create Your Champagne Life

by Cassie Parks

No More Drama: How to Make Peace with Your Defiant Kid

by Lisa Cavallaro

The Nurse Practitioner's Bag: Become a Healer, Make a Difference, and Create the Career of Your Dreams

by Nancy Brook

Farm Girl Leaves Home: An American Narrative of Inspiration and Transformation

by Margaret Fletcher